Wide as God's Love

'The one who prays
will have a heart as wide
as the love of God itself.'

Mother Mary Clare

Wide as God's Love

Edited

by

Jane Osborn and Sr Christine SLG

New City

London Dublin Edinburgh

Published by New City, 1994
57 Twyford Avenue, London, W3 9PZ

A CIP catalogue record for this book is available from the
British Library
ISBN 0 904287 491

Typeset in Great Britain by Phoenix Typesetting, Ilkley, West Yorkshire

Printed and bound in Great Britain by
BPCC Wheatons Ltd, Exeter, Devon

ACKNOWLEDGEMENTS

We are grateful to the following for permission to quote from published
works: James Clarke & Co. Ltd., *The Mystical Theology of the Eastern
Church* by Vladimir Lossky; Darton, Longman & Todd Ltd., *Teach
Us To Pray* by André Louf; HarperCollins Publishers (Harvill), *The
Gulag Archipelago* by Alexander Solzhenitsyn; Penguin Books Ltd. &
Oxford University Press Inc., 'Genesis' in *Collected Poems* by Geoffrey
Hill; Search Press Ltd., *The Spirit of Solzhenitsyn* by Olivier Clément;
Thomas Nelson & Sons, *The Collected Works of St John of the Cross*,
trans. by Kieran Kavanaugh and Otilio Rodriguez; The Community
of the Servants of the Will of God for their translation of 'The
Holy Spirit and Monasticism Today' by Olivier Clément; The Editor
of *Irénikon*, for permission to translate the article from the 1978:2
issue, 'Le Monastère de Saint-Macaire'.

Contents

In thanksgiving for the lives of
Father Gilbert Shuldham Shaw
Mother Mary Clare SLG
and
Sister Marjorie SLG

PREFACE

The Sisters of the Love of God, whose mother house is at Fairacres, Oxford, is a community whose origins go back to the very heart of the Oxford Movement. The two founding fathers of the Community, Father George Seymour Hollings and Father Lucius Cary, were members of the Society of St John the Evangelist, Cowley, and were both, in their different ways, disciples of their own founder, Richard Meux Benson. Benson himself was a direct and devoted disciple of E.B. Pusey, one of the leaders of the Oxford Movement. So from its beginning in 1906 the Community inherited a profoundly balanced, biblical and sane understanding of the Christian tradition and of the contemplative element within it. It was recognized that that tradition is at once one and many.

Father Hollings died suddenly in 1914. the new foundation scarcely established. Father Cary was entrusted with the continuation of his work; as Chaplain General to the Sisters from 1914 to 1950, he therefore profoundly influenced their spiritual formation. He himself had a great affection and empathy for Carmelite teaching, but the spirituality of the Community has never been exclusively Carmelite. It is catholic in a more inclusive sense, open to the Christian east and west alike. Father Cary's friendship with Bishop George Bell brought the Community into direct contact with perhaps the greatest Anglican ecumenist of the years between the two World Wars. And its close and confident relationship with successive bishops of Oxford, from Francis Paget on, has maintained its strong sense of solidarity with the life of the whole Church. Thus the Community has been utterly without that sectarian quality which has at times plagued certain elements within Anglo-Catholicism.

The Community received a new impetus in the inspired partnership of Father Gilbert Shaw, who was Warden of the Community from 1964 to 1967, and Mother Mary Clare, the then

Reverend Mother. In different ways both were convinced not only of the validity of the contemplative life in the eternal sphere, but also of its urgent relevance to the situation of the Church and the world in the last decades of the twentieth century. Mother Mary Clare, in particular, played a prominent part in the two Anglican Religious Life Conferences in Oxford in the 1960s, when communities reassessed their life and work in the light of the changing circumstances brought about by Vatican II. Since that time communities have worked together more closely, and have created new organs of collaboration, such as the Communities' Consultative Council. Active and contemplative communities have a new awareness of both their complementarity and the possibilities of mutual confirmation and support.

If the life of the Sisters of the Love of God has changed in the last twenty-five years, it has been more through a change in the expression of its relationship with the Church and the world beyond its own boundaries than through any dramatic or sudden changes in its own inner life. The Community has entered into closer relationship with guests, retreatants, and associates, and gives strong affirmation to the vocation of its Oblate Sisters. Like all communities in the Church of England it has come to find itself accepted more freely by the whole Church, in all its various traditions, and many look to it for spiritual guidance and teaching. Until the 1960s the women's communities in the Church of England had, to some extent, lived in a world of their own. Since then this has changed greatly. It is difficult to imagine an Archbishop of Canterbury before Michael Ramsey making a retreat in a contemplative community. It would have seemed an unduly 'party-ish' thing for such a person to have done. Since his time, each of his successors has found in the SLG centre in Kent, Bede House, an invaluable place of quiet and retreat.

New contacts have been made not only within the Church of England, but also within the wider Church. Vatican II opened up unimagined possibilities of encounter and exchange with Roman Catholics. The Sisters have made friends amongst the Carmelites, especially in Spain and Germany; amongst Benedictines, for instance, those at Stanbrook and Bec; and amongst Cistercians in Britain, Ireland and the U.S.A. Through her own long-standing friendship with Father Conrad Pepler O.P., Mother Mary Clare developed a particular link with the Dominican centre at Spode House, and some of her most fundamental teaching was disseminated through conferences held there.

The Community has also strengthened its associations with Eastern Orthodoxy, and the presence of notable Orthodox scholars in Oxford, pre-eminent among them Bishop Kallistos of Diokleia, has been important for the Community. Despite the problems of the Cold War, there have been significant contacts with eastern Europe, notably with Romania in the 1970s. Now there is the promise of new openings for dialogue in Russia itself. Father Sophrony of Tolleshunt Knights played an important part in plans for the renewal of the solitary life which developed into the foundation of the 'lavra' at Bede House in 1966.

The recovery of the eremitical life within the Community has been one of the most important aspects of its spiritual growth in the past quarter-century. The solitary way cherishes the elements of silence and hiddenness, and we should respect its specific nature. But it is important to recognize the existence of this way of prayer, and its particular gifts and demands. One of its gifts is the universality of vision which it stimulates.

The deepest of the Community's ecumenical contacts has undoubtedly been with a small Lutheran sisterhood in Germany, Ordo Pacis. Over the years there has been a steady exchange of extended visits between the two communities. Although numerically small, Ordo Pacis was careful to maintain its life both in east and west Germany in the days of political division. In this way the Community came into direct contact with the agonies of a divided Europe.

In the last twenty-five years Christian contemplatives have been thinking and praying not only for the renewal of the Church's unity, but also discovering the underlying reality which unites the diverse traditions of the human family. As the early Christian monks taught, a monk or nun is one separated from all, yet united with all. The meaning of the word 'all' must be constantly rediscovered in a world which has, during this century, become

more and more aware that unity is essential to our survival and
co-existence. We neglect this task at our peril.

We are grateful that in January 1992 the Reverend Robert Farmer
suggested republishing some articles from past issues of the *Fairacres
Chronicle*. For various reasons the book has been delayed and the
seed he sowed has been cultivated by others. This collection
marking the Silver Jubilee of the *Chronicle* is the happy result
of his initial prompting.

Feast of the Transfiguration, 1993   A.M. ALLCHIN
                                                    St Theosevia Centre
                                                          Oxford

Twenty-five Years of the SLG Press

SISTER CHRISTINE SLG

W hen the *Fairacres Chronicle* celebrated its Silver Jubilee in 1992, it was only one of a series of twenty-fifth anniversaries for the Sisters of the Love of God that year. We kept the jubilee of the blessing of Bede House in May 1967, our foundation in Kent, and in August we recalled the death of our Warden, Fr Gilbert Shaw. Bede House, the inspiration of Father Gilbert Shaw and Mother Mary Clare, was founded in the mid-sixties to recover the tradition of desert monasticism for the Church. There a number of hermits live in chalets around a community house. It was originally intended that the SLG Press should operate from these premises. In a 'Memorandum Concerning the Relation of the Solitary to the Coenobitic Chapter' presented by Mother Mary Clare to the Community's Annual Chapter in 1967, there is the following statement:

> Through the generosity of the Warden [Fr Gilbert], who has given us a small litho off-set printing press which is to be set up here at Fairacres ... the work of collating and producing books of spirituality, the writing of reviews and ecumenical conferences, which will be one of the chief works of the Bede House Trust, will begin here at Fairacres with the Warden and Sister Marjorie.

So the work of the Press began, in a tiny room at the Mother House in Oxford, known as Fairacres, with the expectation that Bede House would be its ultimate home. The noise and mess must have been considerable!

In August of that same year, the first *Fairacres Chronicle* was published, as Fr Gilbert lay dying. Indeed, he died before it was finished. It had become evident that something was needed to disseminate Community news and teaching to its many associates, but no one could foresee, nor would have predicted, the substantial journal that evolved. The new foundation and the printing press had a common source, the understanding Fr Gilbert and Mother Mary Clare had of the Community's vocation and how it might be manifested in a time of great change in the Church. The two polarities of that vocation, the call to a hidden life of prayer and solitude, and the furthering of the purposes of Divine Love in the world, were both given new and explicit expression. Hermits and publications are at first sight a surprising combination, but the double movement they signify is, in practice, one of complementarity not contradiction.

By Chapter 1968 Mother Mary Clare was able to report:

> . . . we must humbly realize that we are being turned to more and more for consultation on the themes of renewal and the teaching of prayer. It is with this in view that one looks forward so much to the better conditions for Sister Marjorie to work in in St Gilbert of Sempringham [the print room] at the task of editing and printing Father Gilbert's papers. We have during the year published his intercessory prayers, *Sitio*, and out of the 500 copies printed less than 50 are left. *Fairacres Chronicle* has also been born and three numbers printed and we have received deeply appreciative letters from its readers who now number 700. The Press has also done some other printing and since last September has made a profit in excess of the cost of the materials used of £150.

At the time the reasons for the establishment of a print room at Fairacres, independent of Bede House, were undoubtedly seen as practical. But surely there was a deeper work being wrought by the Holy Spirit in that year between the two Chapter meetings. There is a marked shift from regarding printing and publishing as suitable work for a hermit at Bede House, to justify the aims of the Bede House Trust, to regarding it as an expression of the total community vocation which should be set at the heart of the Mother House. In consequence the implications for each Sister have become important: the Press has never existed only for a few Sisters with editorial or technical skills. The work there springs from the contemplative vocation of the Sisters of the Love of God, expressed particularly through the Eucharist, the Divine Office and personal prayer. Indeed, the Press could not continue without these essential supports.

Both the extracts above mention Sister Marjorie. Those who knew her cannot fail to recognize the tremendous pioneering work she did to establish the Press and to turn it from a print shop into a small publishing house with printing facilities, both to a professional standard. She died in September 1977, and I cannot do better than to quote part of Sr Edmée's 'Tribute to Sister Marjorie' in the Winter 1977 *Chronicle* to give some idea of the person she was and the gifts she brought to this new endeavour.

Sister Marjorie . . . took down Father Gilbert's discourses and reproduced them with a skill and sense of lay-out which greatly assisted the reader's understanding. When, therefore, Father Gilbert expressed the wish that the Community should utilize its resources in the founding of a press for the production and dissemination of Christian literature, it was to Sister Marjorie that the venture was entrusted.

By this time Sister Marjorie was herself fully prepared for the charge. But her remote preparation had begun a few years earlier when, contrary to her private aspirations, one of those moments occurred which, in Sister Marjorie's case, swung her on course for the Press. For many years she had been Infirmarian to the Community and her ultimate hope was that she might test a vocation to the eremitical life. One day, however, a representative from Rotaprint called and Mother Mary Clare collected some likely Sisters to attend the demonstration of the hand-operated machine he was selling. Sister Marjorie was present only under obedience. Her sights were set and men extolling the merits of machinery for reproducing the written word were not in her line of vision. But while the other Sisters stood around silent, in varying degrees of incomprehension, Sister Marjorie's mechanical flair began to operate, and despite herself, she could not help but ask the kind of questions which revealed an immediate grasp of the problems and principles of the piece of machinery under review. Her future was settled.

In later years men trying to sell Sister Marjorie pieces of machinery became a feature of her life. And while she had an all-round ability for every aspect of the Press, from solving a grammatical, stylistic or terminological problem presented by the compositor, to the correct position of the rollers on the Offset Litho, the full extent of her gifts manifested itself most especially in her astute investigations into the capacities of a machine she had decided it was necessary to buy. Many a representative, after spending an hour or two under cross-examination, must have left mopping his brow and wishing he had taken an advanced course in his subject before venturing to put it over to Sister Marjorie, while Sister Marjorie's comment on the afternoon's work, as she tidied away the thumb-screws and lie-detectors, would be: '*Such* a nice man! *So* helpful!'

Now all the printing is done by an excellent local printer, due to a lack of Sisters to spare for this work. Indeed, we have sold the press and platemaker, and do only the editing and typesetting ourselves. But our work of producing and disseminating material on spirituality and prayer has not changed. Our pamphlets are sold all over the world, both through the shop at Fairacres, and by mail order. The *Chronicle* reaches over 1,000 subscribers with every issue, and it is impossible to estimate how many more people see it besides the recipient. As letters received over the years testify, it has become a resource for the spiritual life of many readers, eagerly awaited, with back numbers kept for reference.

Although the three issues of the *Chronicle* per year absorb a great deal of our time, we have also published one hundred and twenty pamphlets of varying lengths, and keep a list of about eighty titles in print. Generally speaking, we reckon to publish short manuscripts which are not economically viable for large commercial publishers, but have value in building up a life of prayer. They are accessible to those who might be daunted by a full length theological book, and a means of whetting their appetites for more. The teaching of Father Gilbert and Mother Mary Clare on contemplative prayer forms the nucleus. However, there is also a strong monastic strand, represented by Sr Benedicta's *The Wisdom of the Desert Fathers*; and a core of Eastern Orthodox spirituality, of which Bishop Kallistos of Diokleia's *The Power of the Name* remains the best seller. This last has been translated into several languages, as have some of the more popular pamphlets on prayer. As I said of the *Fairacres Chronicle*, it is hard to estimate how many people actually read any one of our publications. Recently a customer revealed that he had first met them in a jumble sale!

Religious communities undertake printing and publishing for many reasons, to bring in income or to promote the aims of the order, or both, and tend to develop their talent to full capacity in the process. We come within the second category, and our skills and equipment have greatly improved in twenty-five years. The first *Chronicle* was printed in blue ink from typewritten copy, with the justification accomplished by putting in extra spaces manually within the text − a feat which no compositor would wish to repeat. But in whatever way we develop our talent, we hope that the work of the Press springs from 'true contemplation', described in our Rule as: 'an urgency to love God for himself and . . . a desire that all . . . should be drawn to respond to his mercy'. That is an abiding standard by which to judge our publications, and our own lives.

Sister Christine entered SLG in 1968, and is at present Sister in Charge of the SLG Press.

Held in God's Love

A Tribute to Mother Mary Clare SLG

BISHOP PETER K WALKER (then Bishop of Ely)

With that most generous kindness which I have known from them for over thirty years, and which brings me here today, SLG let me go to be with Mother Mary Clare a little while in that last week. There was a moment of the old affectionate greeting, and then I sat and quietly held her hand.

In a great stillness, in St Teresa's Lodge, a great Religious, a great contemplative, was going to God; and as I quietly left her, her faithful companion, Sister Esther Mary, put into my hand her tiny book, *The Simplicity of Prayer*.[1]

All of her, as I have come to see, is in fact in those few small pages. And I see that as symbolic: almost like the hazelnut in the palm of another great Mother of prayer. The pearl of great price will surely be like this: in an age of many words, words in profusion, words duplicated and tiring to eye and mind alike – instead, this little book transcribed in love, the distillation of a lifetime's prayer, observance, discipline, thought and action.

In her lifetime the world had changed out of recognition. It was changing, on the day she left it in the quietness of St Teresa's Lodge, at a rate we learn in our new language to call 'exponential'. And, thinking as I was towards today, she was somewhere in my consciousness as the Master of a Cambridge College spoke to me, a week ago last night, as a man himself on the frontiers of our knowledge of such things, of the questions we do not know the answer to, or even know that we must ask, about a portent of our day, the ozone gap. All we yet know – and know from the chance of a few men of the Cambridge Antarctic Survey having stumbled on a question – is that a protective shield has been precariously, and irrevocably, punctured. And what else?

Or to take another parable. Others besides herself, she in the quietness of St Teresa's Lodge, and they, for instance, in Ely where the planes from Mildenhall pass low sometimes over the great cathedral, heard one night in 1986 the American engines throbbing on their way to the Libya strike: and were dismayed, hearing echoes from another day in a world with new potential now for a world conflagration.

The point of these two parables is not that these were the times in the world's history she shared with her generation: nor even that here was someone, like other serious-minded men and women of her day, who was deeply concerned. What matters for our remembrance is what these things tell us about what had brought her, in the end, to Fairacres and the life, by day and night, of contemplation.

It was, I think, E.G. Rupp who said a discerning thing of Bishop George Bell's perception of the moment of the saturation bombing of the German cities in the war (and Bell was her own bishop once, her friend and confidant, as were so many of the great churchmen of her time – and, pre-eminently, her dear Michael Ramsey, who 'went' so soon before her). Rupp said that surely Bell was right: the future historian would see that moment as the moment when our world began 'its slow but deadly landslide into all the violence of our present age'. For her, it was the 1941 Cardiff blitz, we know, that brought her to the realization of her distinctive vocation in Religion and to the prayer, particularly, of the night – the prayer of intercessory, reparatory, contemplation. I quote from one of those small pages:

> *for the world's confusion*
> *is held to Calvary in the hearts*
> *of true contemplatives*
> *until all is completed*

and

> *He who prays*
> *stands at that point*
> *of intersection*

> *where the love of God*
> *and the tensions and*
> *sufferings we inflict*
> *on each other*
> *meet and are held*
> *to the healing power of God.*

> *. . . and prayer*
> *which is the fruit of*
> *true conversion is an activity*
> *an adventure – and sometimes*
> *a dangerous one – because*
> *it brings neither peace*
> *nor comfort, but always*
> *challenge, conflict*
> *and new responsibility.*

This, and not less than this, was the dimension given by her to the night we have just remembered.

'Where are the words that have weight?' von Balthasar once asked. You find them in those small pages. The verbs, in particular, for

> *he helps us in the going,*
> *in the doing:*

to *stand*, to *wait*, to *understand* (to *seek* to understand). And the great passives: to be *held*, to be *drawn* – to be drawn into the stillness,

> *not merely into the dark cloud,*
> *but into the tremendous stillness*
> *of the height of Calvary*
> *and through Calvary to the dawn*
> *of the new day . . .*
> *the stillness, the awful stillness,*
> *in which we see the world*
> *from the height of Calvary.*

> *. . . you must learn*
> *to stand at the Cross.*
> *It is a long learning,*
> *a long road, but a sure road,*
> *if it is up the hill to Calvary . . .*
>
> *and through Calvary to the dawn*
> *of the new day.*

It had been a long road, but a sure road: and, in simple truth, only her own God knows *how* much had been held by the prayer of this true contemplative, one might believe the greatest of the contemplatives of our day. And here, then, just here, was the importance *sub specie aeternitatis* of the moment of her passing into her own new day with God.

And this was so human a woman: human, no doubt, as we all are, in some of the mortal frailties, as those who were closest to her in the fragilities of her wearisome last days would know and understand: human as we shall want to remember her, in her twinkle and enjoyment of life. So, in a letter when her dear Sister Elizabeth was 'going to God' (it was the phrase she used of her, so I used it at the beginning of this address today), she had recalled earlier days at Burwash. 'We were all youngish and frisky in those days and had our "holiday" times together. We would lie in the orchard listening spellbound to Wimbledon on the radio – a very dashing form of recreation for "enclosed" nuns in those days!' And this was the spirited daughter of the Principal of Brasenose, who had had the world before her – the girl who, up before the proctors for some breach of University discipline, had paid out her half guinea fine in penny pieces, counted out upon the table one by one with serene effrontery, from the bag of them she had brought in. 'I did, my dear, you know. I did.' The same twinkle, to the end, as she remembered. The same twinkle as when I met her first at Boxmoor: the only time I was late, fractionally, for the celebration (as the young curate, I was normally too nervous to be anything other than ahead of time): 'You're Father Walker: we know all your sins, negligences and ignorances.' ('What would *you*

have said?' I asked my friend Ken Carey. 'My dear, the half was
not told you.' How much she would have loved it if I had.) 'I am
still chirping', she would write in later days, responsive always,
this time to a line I had shared with her from Auden about the
bird who chirped not for effect but because chirping was the thing
to do. The friendly things mattered. That her brother up in Leeds
had prepared my sister for confirmation was a bond. 'Spiritual
direction from her (and so many came to her) was the gentlest
of nudges which you learnt to take seriously.' (So writes Martin
Reith in his affectionate remembrance of her in an intercession
leaflet of the Company of the Servants of God.) So to the
Dean of Chapel of a Cambridge College whose duties, as he
understood them, meant dining with the Fellows most evenings:
'You need a little bit of the desert' – and two days later there
came Dom Lefebvre's *The Well-Springs of Prayer* inscribed in
that surprisingly small hand, 'With SLG's love and prayer', and
below, the two words underlined, *In deserto*. And in the ac-
companying note, 'We hold you in His Love and Prayer *die et
nocte.*'

We shall be thinking of the Trust which will allow religious,
and sometimes the ordinand, a bit of the desert on Bardsey
Island. That will be surely the perfect remembrance. As I sat
that hour with her and absorbed the cell, there were the tidy
books, von Balthasar and the rest (how fresh, how impressive, how
contemporary, to the last, her reading), and there among them
Geoffrey Hill's *Collected Poems*.[2] I kept a letter she once wrote
me, with her words about that first poem in it, the astonishing
poem of the twenty-year-old master: *Genesis*, beginning:

> *Against the burly Air I strode,*
> *Crying the miracles of God.*

and drawing to its last stanza

> *By blood we live, the hot, the cold,*
> *To ravage and redeem the world:*
> *There is no bloodless myth will hold.*

'I have pondered much', she wrote, 'on the poem *Genesis*. So much of it speaks to me of my experience on the Lleyn Peninsula, North Wales, with our hermit sisters. It has been my personal "lifeline" to visit them once or twice a year pastorally. There the death and resurrection cycle seems to be continually enacted whether it be in the crashing waves on the rugged coastline or the gentle murmur of the sea with the ebbing tide. Sometimes it is so still one can just lie and listen to innumerable sounds usually unheard: at other times the buffeting of the gales drowns all other sounds. Equally peace reigns in nature and in one's heart, and then suddenly the heron standing on the sea-shore on one leg seeking his supper is attacked by the swooping wings of an eagle, and a trail of blood on the pebbles is the only sign of his presence left.

> *And where the streams were salt and full*
> *The tough pig-headed salmon strove,*
> *Ramming the ebb, in the tide's pull,*
> *To reach the steady hills above.*

> *The second day I stood and saw*
> *The osprey plunge with triggered claw,*
> *Feathering blood along the shore,*
> *To lay the living sinew bare.*

"Only the suffering God will help" . . . and without the shedding of blood there is no redemption – for in the Blood is the LIFE.'

She was all of a piece. She would like us to look ahead as we remember her. That inclusion of the young, the ordinand, with the religious in the scheme of things, says much. How impressive her concern for, her sympathy with, the young:

Doors are open. Christ is *the* 'door'. Let us not slam the door he is opening to us and to them by making the wrong approaches. These men and women of the younger generation will listen to those who have something to say from their own valid experience . . .[3]

and of this looking ahead:

> *We must try to understand*
> *the meaning of the age*
> *in which we are called*
> *to bear witness.*
> *We must accept the fact that*
> *this is an age in which the*
> *cloth is being unwoven.*
> *It is therefore no good trying*
> *to patch. We must, rather,*
> *set up the loom on which*
> *coming generations may*
> *weave new cloth according*
> *to the pattern God provides.*

She was a woman *on the frontier*. That is why I suppose she was at home at once with the poet on the frontier who might not wholly refuse the relevance to his own poetry of the phrase used of another's, 'a heretic's dream of salvation expressed in the images of the orthodoxy from which he is excommunicate',[4] and with the Professor of Theology of great stature but of too liberal a hue for some, dear Geoffrey Lampe – who, in his last illness, said that he had come to know the tangible reality of her night prayers for him. She had *held* him: as she and SLG would hold his Elizabeth, hoping 'we shall be able to love her through the dark patches'.

On that strong verb I end – *held* in God's love, she held us to him in prayer and affection always: in the deep prayer in which she reached out and from which she reached out, carrying her great Community with her, to hold to God's healing love the world for which Christ died and rose: in the stillness,

the tremendous stillness
of the height of Calvary
and through Calvary to the dawn
of the new day.

And we give thanks for her.

NOTES

1. Fairacres Publication 105.
2. Geoffrey Hill, 'Genesis' in *Collected Poems*, André Deutsch and Penguin Books, 1985.
3. *The Apostolate of Prayer*, Fairacres Publication 23, p.16.
4. *Viewpoints, Poets in Conversation with John Haffenden*, Faber and Faber, 1981, p.98.

Bishop Peter K. Walker was Bishop of Ely from 1977 to 1989. Since his retirement he has acted as an Assistant Bishop in the Diocese of Oxford.

Living through the Dying

The First Reading at the Memorial Service

Any Christian whether living in the world or in the Religious Life, active or enclosed, is being called as was St Antony of old to go down into the most frightening places of world history. If we are really trying to live this life in Christ, we are called to go down into the world situation of today, which is rapidly becoming divorced from God. It is only in prayer that those truly given to God can face this awful sense of disintegration, and face it united to Christ not only in his Passion but also in the power of his Resurrection.

We have got to live now in and through the dying, in order that we may bear witness to the Resurrection life . . . If we live in this glorious perspective, we do not have to wait for the fullness of life after death. Life in God is here and now, experienced first and foremost through experiencing death. Do not be afraid to die, do not be afraid when you are overwhelmed by the sense of your own weakness and sin and muck and desolation. Let everything which is in you, and everything which is thrown up against you by the power of evil, be held in Christ's healing power. Do not absorb it or be overcome by it, but let it in you meet Christ's power to heal; let it in you meet this almighty power of God, so that in you the mess can be transformed, answered.

MOTHER MARY CLARE SLG
From a Conference given to the Community,
Sunday in the Octave of Prayer for Unity, 1968

Transformation into Holiness

Notes from an Address given to the Chapter in 1960

MOTHER MARY CLARE SLG

In Christ we are called to live Christ's way. In so far as that must be expressed in a religion, it is as a religion unique and not to be regarded as modern humanism would have it be, as one religion amongst others and comparable to others. We are reminded in the Epistle to the Ephesians that the inheritance of the Christian is his participation in the consummation of all things and that our incorporation into Christ's body through the sacramental sealing is the earnest of that inheritance:

> Blessed be the God and Father of our Lord Jesus Christ, who has blessed us in Christ with every spiritual blessing in the heavenly places, even as he chose us in him before the foundation of the world, that we should be holy and blameless before him. (Eph. 1:3-4)

The Christian does not discover God, he is found by God to be incorporated into the power of God whereby he is *re-created* a son of God through adoption and grace. In the Incarnation the substance of man's life is taken to be transformed into a wholly new creation. The early Fathers expressed this by saying that 'by the Incarnation man was deified'. This truth of our deification is staggering in its implications. It is in and by the dynamic energy which flows from this transformation that the Christian is perfected, not by the denial of his natural life. Listen to the words of St Paul: 'Do not be conformed to this world but be transformed by the renewal of your mind' (Rom. 12:2). The first image of man deformed through disobedience is transformed by the infusion of the new life of our re-creation in Christ. Our new image is Christ's incarnate life whereby we show forth his death, entering into his dying that we may be transformed into the life of his Resurrection.

Doctrinally we must develop this thought one step further. The work of redemption and transformation wholly proceeds from God, but Christians, both corporately as the body of Christ and individually as members of that body, have their part to play in the reception of and participation in the divine activity. So it is to the source of all unity and holiness that we must look for the fuller realization of the mystery revealed to us in the fullness of time. The Father so loves the world that he gave his Son. The Son so loves the world that he, through his Passion reconciles all things to the Father. The Holy Spirit, the gift proceeding from the Father and the Son to indwell the members of his body, takes of the things of Jesus to show them to the members of the body that they may receive and reflect the image of the perfect humanity from glory to glory. In this world the glory is found and expressed in the following of the Way: 'I am the way, the truth and the life' (John 14:6), and the way leads us to the way of reconciliation whereby through tribulation the kingdom is accomplished in Christ. Christianity, therefore, if it is to meet the basic need of man's spirit, must be a creative spiritual force which has for its end nothing less than the re-creation of all mankind, for the Church is no sect or human organization but a universal new creation in Christ, the seed of the new order which is ultimately destined to transform the world.

Most people have an obscure sense of the existence of a spiritual reality and a consciousness of the evil and misery of an existence which is the slave of sensual impulse and self-interest and which, untransformed, must inevitably end in physical suffering and death. How is man to escape from this wheel to which he is bound by the accumulated weight of his own acts and desires? How is he to bring his life into vital relation with that spiritual reality which transcends all the categories of his thought and the conditions of human experience? This is the fundamental religious problem which has perplexed and baffled the mind of man from the beginning, and which is, in a sense, inherent in human nature.

The religious attitude is only possible in the presence of the eternal and transcendent. The sense of awe and self-surrender is essential to true religion. Only as we realize more and more the meaning of the dependency on God as members of the mystical body which has its true origin and fulfilment in the heavenly, shall we on earth be able to take our full share in God's everlasting reconciliation in order that mankind might once again become a kingdom and a priesthood.

If we as Christians were really alive to the true purpose of our vocation, which is transformation into holiness, then the conquest of the material order by scientific achievement would not offer as it does at present the tragic spectacle of the devotion of vast resources of power and intelligence to the production of unnecessary objects. The recovery of the Christian idea of order would give a spiritual expression to the universality of modern culture, the ideal of the spiritual unity of mankind.

Are we sufficiently aware of the dynamic power that resides in the very fact that we are Christians? Every Christian mind is a seed of change and of potential spiritual power as long as it is a living mind, not enervated by custom or ossified by prejudice. A Christian has only to *be* in order to change the world, for in that very act of being in Christ is contained all the mystery of supernatural life of the renewed creation wrought by the Cross. It is the function of the Church to produce not only good but spiritual men, men made holy by the spirit of God through their incorporation into the living Word himself. And this transformation of each individual is not for the edification of the individual, but for the glory of God, and that all men may be drawn to know the Father. We are all called to the radiant self-communicating power of holiness.

During the course of history, the Church's witness of holiness has assumed a cosmic significance, and in this the development of the religious life has made its own contribution. The contemplative life has always been associated with the principle of withdrawal and ascetic discipline, and those who understand little of this consider it a negative way. We know, however, that the separation of our life, if rightly used, is an essential condition by which our witness of transformation can be offered for the unification and sanctification of the Church and the world.

We must go back, as always, to the Desert Fathers. 'Neither Antony nor Pachomius by their withdrawal step outside history, rather they move from the circumference of history to its centre that God may use them to control history.' That sentence is taken from Derwas Chitty's lectures on the Desert Fathers and it is very significant. The withdrawal and ascetic discipline of the hermit and coenobite was not to avoid activity but to direct and guide the activity into its most completely fruitful channel. It is this one-ing of our energy with the energy of God that is the essence of contemplative prayer. The prayer of the desert may be unseen, but the life of the desert, if it be that which it should be, draws the world to it for inspiration and counsel. By both prayer and witness, this withdrawal of the contemplative life flows back into world affairs to fertilize them with the living waters of the Spirit.

It is very important to realize that historically the desert was sought as a school of sanctity in which the chief lesson was a form of ascetic discipline so that, to quote Fr Chitty again, 'The purpose of the desert as expressed in Antony is for purity of heart, the first stage towards which is an ascesis in which the seeker is first occupied in the renewing of his mind.' This 'renewal of the mind' in our Western terminology could be described as the active form of purgation in the life of prayer. Fr Chitty continues, 'The first stage is followed by a second in which the demons attack Antony from without.' This is the passive purgation of the spirit so vividly, though almost coldly and dispassionately, described by St John of the Cross in *The Dark Night of the Soul*. When this second purification is past, then purity is established, but we must recall the words of one of the Eastern Fathers, Isaac of Syria:

> If the mind desires to mount the Cross before the senses have ceased from their sickness, the wrath of God comes upon it because it has entered on a matter beyond its measure.

Let us pray to the Holy Spirit that we shrink not in generosity
from the training that pure prayer demands, the discipline for
the warfare of God. St Isaac taught that 'The common life
with its ascetic conflict of self-discipline is the bearing of Christ's
sufferings and his Cross', what we might call the way of humble
discipleship, 'and this is the preparation for that further mounting
of the Cross' which he in due time may give us as part of our
sharing with him in the work of reconciliation.

We have already noted that the transformation of the individual
is not for the individual but for the Church and the world. If we
are to be faithful to our vocation to bear witness to the power
of redeeming love, by fidelity and holiness, it can only be by
willingness to pay the cost of the transformation by the Spirit.
It is the power of the Spirit that will unite us as, in deepening
penitence, we pray for the visible unity of the Church. In the
West we have always been prone to invest the Church with the
earthly garments of position and privilege, and it may be that our
Church will never really find her soul until she is willing to be
stripped of the garments of her own prestige, if not actually
bathed in the blood of martyrdom. What we have to offer the
world is a broken body and blood poured out. The nakedness of
the Church is the way to the glorification. The contemplative life
is the way of nakedness and glory.

How we need to pray for vision, for the stillness of the
contemplative in being a participant of eternity brings eternity
into time. Vision means seeing the end in the beginning, seeing
the whole truth as it is in God and not losing our way in the
labyrinths of our own partial sight, seeing the history of man
as a whole, and the nature of man in terms of a single destiny,
seeing always the heights and depths of love, seeing the Cross
as the highest act of God's love.

We must pray for the mind of Christ. Our prayer should be
directed to know God through scripture, and ourselves and the
world in the light of his revelation so that the soul may be
undisturbed and concentrated in its attentiveness and thereby be
a transmitter of God's light. In the words of St Isaac,

True prayer calls for concentration and setting the inner consciousness at rest. There must be serenity of conscience and quietness of mind. This leaves us free to contemplate the new world of Spirit where we renew our inward strength as we actually enjoy converse with God himself.

That rest, that naked intent, can only be secured on the human part – unless God acts by what St Teresa calls 'the short cut' – through the purgation in which the mind is more and more concerned to meditate on the things of God, and the emotional life directed without reservation to the desire and doing of the will of God, the keeping of the commandments that God may dwell in the soul that he is transforming.

Love and sacrifice must gather all into the unity of the divine energy so that our will and his purpose are one. Christ reigns, he has broken down the middle wall of partition, he is our peace. Let us not be disobedient to the heavenly vision, that we may know the measure of the wisdom which he wills for us.

Mother Mary Clare was Mother General of the Sisters of the Love of God from 1954 to 1973. Until her death in 1988, she was in much demand as a spiritual adviser and counsellor.

A New Beginning

Our Lady's Place in the Scheme of Redemption

GILBERT SHAW

The recovery of a simple, natural, unforced devotion to our Lady is important as being both the clarification and protection of the saving fact of the Incarnation of our blessed Lord. Our salvation begins with the childbearing of the blessed Virgin Mary, for she is prepared by God for his tremendous act of redemption when the Eternal Word takes the flesh that she provides.

The blessed Virgin Mary is brought into being in the natural order 'in the fullness of time', to quote the opening words of the Epistle to the Hebrews, to be under the providence of God the means by which the act of God restores what man had lost through sin. Man had lost the simple dependence needed to fulfil the will of God, the purpose of his creation. We are so saturated with our self-will that we are unable to recognize the wonder of the simple 'so be it' of our Lady, for it is utterly contrary to the response of sinful fallen humanity. She is greeted by the angel as 'Blessed above all women' – blessed because she was full of grace, blessed in her perfect dependence upon the divine will. There is a new fact in history: the coming into being in the flow of the natural course of historic progress, of a creature who will completely recognize her state of dependence as the creature and give her free assent wholly (body, soul and spirit) to God's will for her and for humanity. Here is no idealism or philosophic speculation but a material fact.

William Temple is recorded as saying that Christianity is the most material of all religions. It is not a theory or a philosophy whereby the soul can escape from the burden of the body. It is the Christian revelation of God's mercy to man that takes the body and makes it whole. That is the uniqueness of Christianity: not only our faith in Christ as Person, but in Christ as the Redeemer of the whole man; Christ not as an example but as Life. He takes the manhood through the obedience of the human mother to inaugurate and work out in time and in history the Chosen People. In her the promise to Abraham is fulfilled. She gathers into herself the wholeness of human history that she might be the answer to God's call, the answer that man ought to give, that man was created to give, the answer of utter obedience.

As in the first creation the Holy Spirit overshadowed the nothingness of chaos, so in the re-creation it is the Holy Spirit that overshadows the obedience of the innocency of complete dependence which allows him to do and to work the fullness of his will – the re-creation whereby Christ is incarnate in the flesh of man.

St Jerome in his commentary on the first verse of chapter one of St Matthew's Gospel draws a clear distinction, and one which we must not forget, between the generation of the Eternal Son in the mystery of the Trinity, and the humanity of Christ, the physical child of Mary, yet one Person, Christ, God and Man.

> We read in Isaiah, 'Who shall declare his generation?' We must not, therefore, think that the Evangelist is contrary to the Prophet because that which the one said was impossible of statement, the other begins to relate. One is speaking of the generation of the Godhead, the other of the Incarnation. But he begins from mortal persons, that we may learn to know God through man.

The difficulty for many today, as for many in the early Church, is to hold two apparently illogical inconsistencies together. How can God, absolutely perfect in himself, be man? God has given the answer and we hold the two apparent inconsistencies together in the mystery of the Incarnation.

We must see that our Lady is a necessity of man's salvation, and also a necessity of history in the actual fact of the historic birth of the Word. She is Mother of God in his humanity. This again is a difficulty for man. Man is so caught up in the whole question of evolution. It is quite true things do evolve; man is becoming more proficient, is getting more control of his environment and more power over other men. The natural evolution of politics, economics, science and everything else can go on, but the Way and the Truth of re-creation has come into time once and for all to sanctify all time. We must look to the end, but the end is here. Mary has borne Jesus; he is the result of the re-creation of humanity and of each individual, body, soul and spirit, who is gathered into his body. Our blessed Lady is brought into that mystery; the humanity of Christ is flesh of Mary. The early Church clearly realized that in generally giving her the title of Second Eve.

If there is to be a re-creation, there must be that which can be re-created. The beginning of creation is a beginning of life out of nothing, but re-creation must be of that which has already been created. It is not an evolution of the condition of that which had fallen away from its first purpose, but a new beginning – the re-creation of the first purpose.

The fallen is so sin-conditioned that it needs to be washed. It needs to be restored through the giving of its will to be restored. It is washed by the blood-shedding; it is restored in the New Adam. What is necessary is the re-fashioning, the transfiguration of that which could be re-created: the wholeness of man as God willed man to be. In the sinlessness of the new creation Christ alone could satisfy the wholeness of the result of the disobedience and falling short wherein all men should be drawn, brought back to be sons of God through adoption, not by any merit that lay in man, but solely by the mercy of God who was made the new man. Christ was so completely man that he could be tested as every fallen man is tested. As sinless, he could bear all sin and so triumph over death, for death as we know it, is the penalty for falling short of the Divine purpose. Death could not hold the humanity of the Incarnate, yet in the inconceivable mercy of taking the manhood from Mary, the Incarnate Son could suffer every pain and degradation that is possible to humanity. Only the Sinless could endure the reality of being tested to the limit so that he made the satisfaction for the sin of the world.

This is Love's mystery; God so loved the world that he gave the Eternal Son to be the propitiation for our sin. It is a free act of

God and it asks a freedom of response from man. It is necessary that natural humanity should make the answer: the answer of the 'Be it unto me' of our Lady, wherefore she is full of grace. She is full of grace. She is born in the whole context of the providential working out of history for that purpose, gathering into herself by the grace of God the totality of the consummation of human purpose, for he is Way, Truth and Life, Source, Guide and Goal, 'for of him and through him and to him are all things' (Rom. 11:36).

The fact of the motherhood establishes the reality of bodily redemption; it gives the objective standard for our faith. It is not a case of speculation. We are not given Christ as an ideal of a free man in whom to believe, nor as a demonstration of God's love whom we ought to copy. Faith is never fully faith unless it is realized in love. God's love and our Lady's obedient love give newness of life to those who believe that they may return love, and in returning love be increased in faith. Faith requires us to throw ourselves completely in utter trust on what God is and on what God has done. We must have faith in the Person who is and who was in time; who at a moment in time was born, at a moment in time was crucified, at a moment in time rose from the dead, at a moment in time ascended into the heavens, and who will come again to bring time to an end. He is so closely connected with our blessed Lady that she cannot be separated from him, wherefore we cannot help but love her as we love him.

We aim to follow Christ that we may stand with our Lady at Calvary in the unity of dependence and of willing acceptance of suffering:

> that I may know him and the power of his resurrection, and the fellowship of his sufferings, being made conformable unto his death; if by any means I might attain unto the resurrection of the dead.
>
> (Phil. 3:10-11)

The *consummatum est* of Calvary is wholly the work and the suffering of Christ; the complete reconciliation of manhood with God as Christ through death destroys death and overcomes the evil that causes death, the evil which is the enemy of man's fulfilment of dependence on God. Death is the last enemy to be overcome at the final end when the reign of Christ is gathered up into the final offering of all things to the purposes of God. Love holds the dependence of Mary ever blessed and the few with her standing at the Cross as faithful witnesses of Christ's physical death. To stand at the Cross is the prelude to the experience of union with Christ's resurrection body, to receive the knowledge and power to be his witnesses, to become, through the grace of union with his eternal life, living members of his Body whereby his love can be mediated to all men. Mary suffers the fulfilment of the prophecy of Simeon and she must know the pain of temporal separation. Mary and those with her, the faithful few, do not die with our blessed Lord at Calvary. Mary goes on living in the Church; she knows the waiting for Pentecost; she is the Mother of John by our Lord's own decree; she mothers the Early Church in the Upper Room.

Mary is the model of our life as members of the Church of God. We must know with her the sword of pain because the sin of the world pierces our very heart. We must know with her the prayer of being in Christ's drawing of all things to unity through his suffering of all the woes, sins and limitations of fallen humanity. We must know that re-creation is only possible through the total re-direction of self when self can echo Mary's 'Be it unto me' – Mary's acceptance of her part in God's merciful re-creation.

Let us never forget the fact, the physical fact of the Incarnation. We commemorate it in the last of the responses at the Night Office of the Feast of our Lady's Nativity: 'I know not how to praise thee, for thou hast borne in thy breast him whom the heavens cannot contain.' 'Thou hast borne in thy breast', that is a physical fact, we might say, a biological fact. Herein is the wonder of the human frame: God has had mercy on it; God has clothed himself with the humanity which we share. We should reverence our body because God who is beyond time, beyond space, beyond everything, thought it possible to take human flesh, the flesh that was the veil of the innocency and purity of the complete dependence of our blessed Lady. That innocency and purity of complete dependence we must learn from her. We must reverence our body, for however much the physical may change, as it is always changing – passing away dust to dust – it is the material in which our soul is being prepared to be wholly obedient to know the vision of God.

We do not know what it will be when the wholeness of each and the unity of all is gathered in the final harvest of life's purpose, when body, soul and spirit are united for ever into one obedience, but our trust is that through the grace of Christ and in the fellowship of the Spirit, we who believe are even now the sons of God, 'and every man that hath this hope in him purifieth himself, even as he is pure' (1 John 3:3).

Love realized in obedience is the factual basis of re-creation and of spiritual progress. All the Fathers, Justin, Tertullian and, in particular, Irenaeus, to mention but a few, speak of our Lady as the Second Eve, for in her the whole history of man is gathered up. It is well to think of this in these days when we compare the Christian revelation of the Word of Truth with the speculations and search for God of the Hindu and Buddhist.

We have faith and life, sacramental life, because God has acted in the natural. We are baptized into his Body whereby our body is sanctified and the wholeness of man is re-created by being drawn into Christ's perfect re-creation. By the Incarnation God redeems the material world from its isolation from spirit; and to confirm the reconsecration of matter, he rises from the dead and ascends into heaven in the bodily form. We affirm that Christ's Incarnation, once and for all, closes the gap that exists between soul and body which had kept the latter in perpetual subjection to death. Christ's body, the flesh he took from Mary, was not able to be subject to death because it was sinless.

It is that life which Christ gives to his members that through death they may share his life – life eternal.

> Changed we shall certainly be [through resurrection] but changed because purged from sin, and therefore incorruptible, but not deprived of our creaturely individual being which is God's unique gift to us. For entrance into the Christian heaven does not entail loss of personality, but its infinite enrichment in communion

and union not only with God through Christ, but also with all our fellow men in what is called the Communion of Saints.[1]

We come to that blessedness of union as individuals. The blessed Mary remains Mary, Mother of Jesus, Mother of God. Blessed John remains John. Heaven is a sphere of perfect relationship, the relationship which is looking to the end in Christ. As Christ's members, we must learn both to live that relationship and to bring it into the life of man's earthly pilgrimage.

Herein is the conflict. Herein also is the wonder of being a Christian: death does not separate, for sin is separation; but in Christ we are in union with all who are in Christ. St John of the Cross tells us:

> Mine are the heavens and mine is the earth; mine are the people, the righteous are mine and mine are the sinners. The angels are mine, and the Mother of God and all things are mine and God himself is mine and for me, for Christ is mine and all for me. What then dost thou ask for and seek, my soul? Thine is all this and it is all for thee.[2]

These words express the mutuality of love to all that are in Christ – our Lady, the saints, the living and each other – praying that there should be perfect peace and unity amongst all, and the perfection of the 'Be it unto me according to thy will'.

As we commemorate the fact of our union with one another in Christ, we ask the prayers of each other, and so quite simply we ask our Lady, Mother of God, to pray for us, just as we would ask any other friend. So too we ask the whole company of heaven for their prayers. This is not slipping into some pagan thought; we are all in Christ and are friends together in Christ.

> It can be no detraction from the worship and praise of Almighty God to realize that there is a great company that praises and worships him, which has passed by the same way that we are traversing in this present time. Earthly worship is not the only worship that ascends to God. Our worship on earth can only be a very poor reflection of that perfect adoration in the heavenly

places where saint answers saint in ceaseless praise. If that is so, and if we believe in 'the communion of saints', we should not fear to recognize the fact and rob our prayers of the truth we assert in the Creed . . . To omit devotions wherein our Lady and the saints find a fitting place would deny Christian tradition. Naturally and properly a devotion to our Lady will take first place, but after that each individual will find his own special friendships, attachments, and devotion. It is natural to our loneliness and fitting to our humility to ask the prayers and care of our friends. It would indeed be unneighbourly if we restricted this operation to the limited circle of those whom we could know in the flesh, and ignored the number of those whom we might come to know by faith.[3]

We thank God for being in the family of God wherein our blessed Lady is truly our Mother and the saints are our friends.

Our Lady is the pattern of Christian life in her perfect obedience to God's grace to return in faith the fullness of love, a fullness of love which if we are in Christ we, as good children of a good Mother, should learn from her. She is the Mother of all Christians because she is the Mother of Christ in whom we are. We must learn from her so that being recovered from our natural deformation of self-will, we may respond to grace and so be offered wholly to the Father in the Son's obedience, being overshadowed by the Holy Spirit for renewing of life and increase of grace. That is our place in the conflict of life: to fulfil the will of God in Christ through the fellowship of the Holy Spirit.

NOTES

1. R.C. Zaehner, *At Sundry Times*, p.191.
2. *Spiritual Sentences*, 25.
3. From the Introduction to *A Pilgrim's Book of Prayers*, Mowbray, 1945 reprinted SLG Press, Oxford, 1992.

Father Gilbert Shaw served among the unemployed in Poplar in the 1930s and later at St Anne's, Soho. For many years he worked for the Association for Promoting Retreats. He was Warden of the Sisters of the Love of God from 1964 until his death in 1967.

Father Gilbert Shaw

FATHER GREGORY CSWG

This year has brought us to the twenty-fifth anniversary of the death of Fr Gilbert Shaw, on 18 August 1967. Most of us who knew him during those last fruitful years of his life at Fairacres were somewhat overawed by the might of his holiness and the richness of his teaching. Nevertheless, we were convinced that what he taught had a special ring of truth about it; and what he was saying then seems in retrospect even more obviously relevant to the situation of the Church now.

It is difficult, however, to give a résumé of his teaching, or even to know where to begin, for as well as being a person with a unique clarity of understanding of the new life in Christ, he was someone of unusually wide experience, interests, and reading. He always had something interesting and informative to talk about!

The Restoration of the Church

Yet because this is something of a memorial to a prophet sent by God to speak to the urgent needs of our times – a prophetic word which still needs to be more widely heard – I will begin by quoting his meditative poem 'Glastonbury', which shows the direction in which his hopes lay. It begins with a quotation from Ezekiel 36:36: 'I the Lord build the ruined places, and plant that which was desolate'.

> That which was wasted
>   will be restored
> as Love gives love.

Man cannot hasten
   that which will be
   except by prayer,
true prayer in union
   with Love's creation
   to build afresh
that which man's folly
   did break and mar
   in pride of self.

Life flows in healing
   with every prayer
   that is of truth,
when self is given
   in abandonment
   that Love may rule.

Then is the glory
   not the work of man
   but all God's love:
to whom be glory
   in perfect power
   now and evermore
from all creation.

This poem shows Fr Gilbert as a prophet of the restoration of the Church. He saw the Church as having become assimilated in its outward structures to the social, political and economic life of European Christendom, a Christendom which had now come under the judgement of God for having largely failed to produce the goods of Christianity for the people of the world. The shakable things were now being shaken, so that the unshakable foundations of the Church might be exposed for a work of rebuilding its common life and prayer, in order to serve the purposes of God within the existing state of the world.

The problem has always lain in man's will to build according to his own ideals so as to be able to express himself in action. Hence the present need first to recover true dependence upon God: 'Man cannot hasten/that which will be/except by prayer,/true prayer in union/with Love's creation . . .' For, in building to serve his own temporal ideals, man had broken or marred much of the true pattern of the Church's life and faith.

It was with this understanding in heart and mind that Fr Gilbert approached all questions of renewal. He was fully appreciative of the great work undertaken over the last century by scholars in biblical studies, patristics, and liturgy, which he regarded as necessary for any practical renewal of Church life; therefore he was always helping to build up our libraries and recommending books for study. Yet it was his awareness that at the level where God himself is acting, in ourselves and in our common life, the way ahead must always pass through the paschal mystery of Christ's death and resurrection, that led him to put the primary emphasis on prayer, solitary and corporate. At that level, precisely because it is God who is acting, we don't know initially what is happening to us and cannot understand until Christ himself gives us something of the wisdom of the cross. Moreover, we cannot plan our way ahead: we need to take up the cross obediently as God offers it to us in the unfolding circumstances of life.

In this way Fr Gilbert came to have profound appreciation of the apophatic dimension of theology, as found especially in the Eastern Fathers of the Church. We need from theology both the positive affirmation of the great facts of God's work in creation and re-creation in Christ, and also those apophatic aspects of theology which protect us from the sort of false ratiocination which would lead us back to the world, back to self-motivated planning and action. The necessary task of prayer is to take our troubled situation to God and accept lovingly to be crucified and die to self within it, so as to wait upon him for the emergence of new life, through 'Love's creation/to build afresh/that which man's folly/did break and mar/in pride of self'. Such was his understanding of the new life which 'flows in healing/with every prayer/that is of truth/when self is given/in abandonment/that Love may rule'.

The Contemplative Life of Prayer

It was this aspect of witness to Christ – 'following the naked Christ nakedly' – through the way of the cross so that new life might 'flow in healing' which brought Fr Gilbert into close kinship with the spiritual masters of the Western Church, who had also understood the increase of prayer as God's way of repairing the Church. He had a special love for the Celtic saints who were the foundation stones of the Church in our own land. Amongst later authors he drew especially upon St Catherine of Siena, the Flemish mystic Ruysbroeck, St Teresa of Avila, and St John of the Cross. Yet it was his own personal experience of the way of purgation, illumination and union as described by St John of the Cross and others, and his sharing of it with the numerous people he directed, which brought him to an awareness of the essential unity of the spiritual traditions of the Eastern and Western Church in their most mature exponents. In both traditions the unitive way was to be experienced as a growing realization of the prayer of Jesus in John 17:11: 'Father, I pray that they may be one as we are one'. Fr Gilbert came, therefore, to speak of the 'recovery of the One Great Tradition' of the Church's spiritual life, and he saw this as the appropriate aim of all who take the life of prayer seriously.

Because Fr Gilbert saw Christian spiritual life thus, as having its roots in our sacramental incorporation into Christ our Great High Priest, who reigns with the Father in the glory of the Holy Spirit, all his later spiritual writings have a strong eschatological flavour. In all the trials coming to us as Christians we are exhorted to look to the End: 'Lift up your heads, for your redemption is drawing nigh' (Luke 21:28).

The Christian contemplative life is lived in the light of the present *parousia* of Christ, in expectation of his final coming to inaugurate the new creation, a new heaven and a new earth. Paradoxically, it is this living in the light of the end, Christ glorified with the Father, which brings the disciple into an ever deeper realization of the cross. For it is in the light of Christ that self-knowledge is given and repentance and dependence upon the Holy Spirit become more real; and it is the Spirit alone who can empower the penitent to stand in and unite himself with the self-oblation of Christ on the cross.

The increase of faith, hope, and love, which God freely gives to his penitent and dependent servants, infuses the desire to participate in that sole means of taking away the sin of the world: the cross and passion of our Lord Jesus Christ. The one who has drawn his servant into the light of his glory then takes him down into the dark places of man's sinful separation from God. By this witness the servant strengthens others who are taking up the cross of the spiritual conflict, which they too must suffer in order to be drawn into the light of Christ.

Hence the alternations of light and darkness, of oppressive suffering and praiseful joy, which are experienced by those who are following Christ in the way of contemplation. The way of advance has to be a constantly affirmed 'Yes' to God in times of trial, until there is no preference for light or darkness, refreshment or suffering; indeed until there is nothing left of a shadow of doubt in the mind, or a lack of love in the will which the dark powers could latch on to. The aim of the contemplative intercessor, in the simplicity of his 'Yes' to God in all that comes to him, is, then, to 'put love in where love is not' (St John of the Cross), so that God may be glorified in all the affairs of mankind.

The Unity of Tradition

It was through his own experience of this spiritual conflict leading to 'the light of the knowledge of the glory of God in the face of Jesus Christ', as expounded by the Western spiritual masters, which enabled Fr Gilbert to meet with mutual understanding contemporary exponents of the Eastern Orthodox tradition and to discern the points at which the two traditions, with their different terminologies and variations of practice in the earlier stages, come together. This is the stage at which the action of God in the givenness of contemplative prayer begins to predominate over man's efforts to gather and offer himself through spiritual disciplines aided by divine grace. This is expressed in St John of the Cross by the night of the senses, and in the Eastern Fathers by the life of active practice for overcoming the passions.

Fr Gilbert recognized that the positive content of the *nada* of the passive night of faith in St John of the Cross is similar in significance to the *apatheia* of the Eastern tradition. He saw, too, the great value for grasping the underlying unity of both traditions of St Gregory Palamas's exposition of the theological basis of the life of contemplation, in which the unknowable essence of God is to be distinguished from his self-revealing energies. These are the same divine energies in which the cosmos is created and sustained and in which it is brought to its final goal by the redeeming work of Christ and the ongoing witness of his servants in his body, the Church. When we pray in the Lord's Prayer, 'Your will be done', we are opening ourselves to the inflow of the divine energies, so that we may flow out of self in the same energies to serve for accomplishing the divine purpose for creation. Since the divine energies are precisely the living God in action, there can be no question of man harnessing these energies for his own use. Rather, to open ourselves to the action of the will of God upon ourselves in this way is to suffer and die with Christ and so enter into his resurrection life, which is the beginning and assurance of the new creation to come (cf. 1 Cor. 15:22-5).

In both the Eastern and Western traditions the earlier stages of spiritual life consist of the active practice of the commandments of Christ and the theological virtues, based on meditation on the word of God and obedience to the spiritual father within the common faith and prayer of the Church community, ordered as an 'ascetical community', or a 'training school' for the Christian life. The monastic community serves as a witness to the Church concerning this essential aspect of its own common life.

Synergy

Through this active practice, the Eastern Fathers aim for a growing 'synergy', or an 'energizing' of the human will in union with the divine will and energy. This 'synergy' can also be described as a co-operation between man and God in the Holy Spirit. Since the word 'co-operation' has an active sense in English, these elements within the 'synergy' of repentance and dependence upon the Spirit need to be strongly emphasized so as to keep to and affirm the primacy of the divine action. There should be first of all a freely-willed surrender of the self through the death and resurrection of Christ, from which can then flow an effective active co-operation, as directed by the Holy Spirit, for building up the Church in unity and love.

In the higher levels of contemplation, the mutual self-giving of man and God in Christ enables the fire of the Holy Spirit to effect a transfiguration of the human nature so that man becomes a partaker of the divine nature. Man is destined to participate in the divine light which radiated from Christ on Mount Tabor.

As increasingly more spiritual writings from the Eastern Orthodox tradition became available during the 1950s and 1960s, Fr Gilbert was enabled to set his own spiritual teaching, drawn from the Western spiritual masters, within the firm theological framework which the Eastern tradition provided. In his own realization of the One Great Tradition underlying the long-separated traditions of East and West, he saw a wonderful complementarity between the two. On the one hand, he saw the need to complement a too activist interpretation of the synergy of the Holy Spirit, to which the modern Christian is always liable, with the classical Western understanding of a progression from 'active' to 'passive' purgation. On the other hand, he saw the difficulty which the Easterners have with the notion of a 'passive' purgation, since for them 'passivity' means a 'passion' to be overcome through the practice of *apatheia*, so that there can be a unified response in the synergy of the Holy Spirit. He saw that the Western notion of 'passivity' needed to be set within an explicit affirmation of the action of the Holy Spirit in drawing out the human response of faith ('Jesus Christ is Lord') and love ('Abba, Father').

Undoubtedly, St John of the Cross is wholly trinitarian in his teaching about the spiritual life. Yet, by drawing on the Eastern Fathers, Fr Gilbert found a more clearly formed theological framework within which to express this Western tradition of spiritual growth.

Without exaggeration, one could say that Fr Gilbert brought to a practical resolution a methodology which had been characteristic of Anglican theology since the Reformation. Beginning with Hooker and Andrewes and continuing through the line of the Caroline Divines and their successors in the Oxford Movement up to Michael Ramsey, Anglican theologians had sought to transcend the almost exclusive Western theological dependence upon St Augustine by drawing extensively upon the Eastern Church Fathers. Yet, as long as this search was pursued mainly at the level of dogmatic theology, along with an interest in forms of liturgy, there continued to be in Anglican theology what Michael Ramsey described in *The Gospel and the Catholic Church* as a 'certain archaic flavour'.

Yet the Eastern Fathers themselves were monks and men of prayer whose theological writings and liturgies came out of a knowledge of the living God, the Holy Trinity. By opening up for us a way from our Western spiritual tradition into that of the Eastern Fathers, Fr Gilbert brings the whole of that tradition alive for us in the present, so that our use of it loses its 'archaic flavour' and we become with him receptive to the wonder of the whole economy of salvation. We begin to discern its operation in our own times and our own particular place for co-operation within it. We find that the Fathers are not separated from us by a long gap in time. They reign with Christ and can speak to us in the Spirit through their writings now.

Indeed, I would go so far as to suggest that, if we are to look for a particular vocation for the Anglican Church in its history of temporary separation from the rest of the Western Church, we will find it in this search for the recovery of the one tradition of the Church and the possibility this opens up of rediscovering a 'grass-roots catholicism' of the local Church community. In making the Fathers and their writings contemporary for us in this living way, Fr Gilbert is shown to be himself a latter day Father of the Church.

Prophetic Prayer

It was this realization of the one living tradition of the Church, laid open to us now, which produced such strong cosmic and prophetic emphases in Fr Gilbert's teaching on contemplative prayer. Christian prayer has nothing in common with the many techniques offered by contemporary gurus for attaining self-realization or self-transcendence, though these techniques are often called 'contemplation'. True contemplation is an offering of the human will and energy to Christ to be made spiritual in the Holy Spirit, and so united with the one purpose of God for drawing his creation back to himself. The goal is a new creation, the kingdom of God. Thus contemplative prayer serves for the completion of God's creative purpose for the whole cosmos, and never a merely subjective purpose.

At the very heart of this creative work of God is the sending of his incarnate Son to free creation from the bondage of human sin, which would otherwise hinder it from returning to its source and goal in God. Therefore, contemplation begins with man's welcoming of Christ, who comes to his chosen servants for judgement and mercy to stir up their response of repentance and faith. This obedient response of the servants of God, in turn, brings the light of judgement upon the world with which they unite themselves; and it prepares the way for for final coming of the Lord. Within their own sphere of witness they are given the prophetic word to announce with conviction the revelation of the Holy Trinity as the source and goal of creation. Hand in hand with the prophetic gift comes the divine economy to minister salvation, and to declare the judgements of God on mankind's failure, individual and corporate, to hear and to obey the word of God which has been addressed to them.

Within his general concern for the recovery of the Church's One Great Tradition of contemplative prayer and life, Fr Gilbert had a special concern for the welfare of the Church's two traditional forms of consecrated life: the priesthood, and the religious life with its heart in the monastic withdrawal. He saw both of them as witnessing to that total commitment within the body of Christ

which was implied for every Christian by his baptism. In his 1962
retreat, *Consecration*, preached at Fairacres, he said:

> We stand as witnesses, or as St Paul says, 'God's ambassadors to
> plead with the world: Be reconciled to God.' That is why there
> is such an undercurrent of pressure of seduction against religious
> and against the priesthood which is noticeable as we review the
> signs of the times.

What the religious express in the total offering of life through
the monastic Rule, the priest offers through presiding over the
liturgical and sacramental life of the Church. His consecration is
an identification with Christ the Head and High Priest of the
Church so that the spiritual energies of the kingdom of God
might flow forth to draw his people and overcome evil.

Fr Gilbert had a wonderful capacity as celebrant of the eucharist
to draw the whole assembly into a unified offering by means of
his own recollection and unity of self-giving by, with, and in
Christ. He always took to the altar with him a little prayer
book in which were written his principal mass intentions. They
were also the intentions of his life:

1. To be in our Lord's drawing of all things to the Divine
   Unity.
2. To pray for and teach the recovery of the great tradition of
   prayer, and especially to support and instruct the contemplatives in the world and the religious life.
3. To pray for the increase of vocations to the priesthood and
   the religious life, especially for CSWG and SLG.
4. To pray and suffer for holiness for all men everywhere,
   but especially for the priesthood.
5. To stand and go on standing in our Lord's overcoming
   and in his reversal of evil.

Perhaps it is these Mass intentions which give us the clearest
insight into the life of this great priest. His whole life had become
one offering with Christ in the eucharist; and the same light

and power of healing as is manifested and communicated in the eucharist was operative in his teaching and spiritual direction. So it is greatly to be hoped that more of his writings will become available to feed the spiritual needs of these times, the famine of the hearing of the word of God of which he often reminded us, and which he sought to redress by his teaching and prayer.

Father Gregory is the Superior of the Community of the Servants of the Will of God, Crawley Down, in whose foundation Father Gilbert Shaw played a large part.

Wholeness and Transfiguration

Illustrated in the lives of St Francis of Assisi and St Seraphim of Sarov[1]

A.M. ALLCHIN

In the past century Anglicans have sometimes thought of the recovery of the religious life as the supreme vindication of the catholicity of the Church to which they belong, and surely not without justification. But perhaps more deeply we can think of it as an implicit affirmation of the unity of the Church across the barriers which at present divide us from one another. It is an affirmation that the heritage of the first centuries is still a vital reality in the Church today, that St Antony and St Pachomius, St Benedict and St Basil, St David and St Columba are living powers within our own Church, as they are within the Church of Rome or the Church of Eastern Orthodoxy. An affirmation that this unity is particularly realized and declared when the Churches live from the power of the Spirit, in complete dependence on Jesus Christ our Lord; when our faith in the holiness of the Church, its participation in the divine life, ceases to be a formula which we repeat and becomes an experienced reality of daily life.

So it is that the founders of our communities would have been, I believe, in deep accord with the Russian Metropolitan in Paris between the two wars, Metropolitan Eulogy, when he declared, 'Men like St Seraphim, St Francis of Assisi and many others have in their lives accomplished the union of the Churches. Are they not citizens of the same holy and universal Church? At the level of their spiritual life they have gone beyond the walls which divide us, but which, in the fine expression of Metropolitan Platon of Kiev, do not reach up to heaven.'[2] Not only in the lives of the great saints, though there pre-eminently, but wherever the life of prayer is being truly and authentically lived, there the unity of the Church is being made known, through the healing action of the Holy Spirit. There too is revealed another kind of unity, that which exists between different expressions of the religious or monastic ideal, a unity which makes that diversity a source of enrichment, not of narrowness or division. One of the lesser known figures of the twelfth-century monastic revival in France affirms this clearly:

> In my Father's house there are many mansions, and there are many ways which lead to it. These various ways have been commended in writing by divers of the Fathers, and they are called the Rules of St Basil, St Augustine and St Benedict. These are not the sources of the religious life, but only its offshoots, they are not the root but the leaves. The Rule from which all others derive, like streams flowing from a single source, is the Holy Gospel.[3]

What I want to do in this essay is to examine this assertion of unity a little more closely in relation to precisely the two saints mentioned by Metropolitan Eulogy, St Francis and St Seraphim. I believe that we shall find that the unity of which they tell us is not only an ecclesiastical unity in the narrow sense of that word. Rather it is a unity, an integration of each one of us within himself, and also a unity, an integration of each one of us with all our fellow men, and indeed with all creation. It is only when man begins to rediscover himself as both microcosm, the one in whom the world is summed up, and mediator, the one through whom the world is offered to God, that the divisions of the Churches will begin to be healed. For only in such a perspective are the true dimensions of human unity revealed, and its Godward direction made plain. The unity for which our Lord prays is based in God himself; it is a unity which is for all men and not against them, for all creation and not against it, since God himself is Father, Redeemer, and Sanctifier of all.

In coming to understand the nature of this work of unification, this restoration of wholeness, I believe we have something to learn from those, some of them outside the Churches, who in our own century have studied man's nature at depth in the school of Carl Gustav Jung. They help the theologian to give flesh and blood to concepts and traditions which are in danger of remaining dis-incarnate, too exalted to be rooted in man's creatureliness. Thomas Merton, for instance, in his essay on 'Final Integration', in *Contemplation in a World of Action*, makes extensive use of the work of a Persian psychiatrist, versed both in the practice of depth psychology and in the Sufi tradition of discipline and prayer. He re-opens for us an understanding of what it means to find that the human person, when approaching the fullness of life and being, becomes catholic, universal. The fully integrated man 'is in a certain sense "cosmic", and "universal man". He has attained a deeper, fuller identity than that of his limited ego-self which is only a fragment of his being. He is in a certain sense identified with everybody, or in the familiar language of the New Testament . . . he is "all things to all men".'[4] He is freed from the limitations of a particular cultural tradition, though not uprooted from it. He no longer has to affirm his identity against others. He can be *for* everyone.

A very similar affirmation is to be found in a book written by a French Franciscan in exposition of St Francis's great poem, 'The Canticle of the Creatures'. In this remarkable work, Fr Eloi Leclerc contends, in a way which reveals a clear influence of Jungian ideas, that St Francis's celebration of the creatures, sun and moon, earth and air, fire and water, life and death, is not only an act of acknowledgement of the created world around him, but also of the unconscious depths within, of the great archetypal powers which lie within us. In this way the author reactivates the ancient idea of man as a microcosm, and of a correspondence between man's inner world and the outer world in which he is placed. 'In opening himself to the world, in taking his place among the creatures, in becoming profoundly aware of them as "brothers" and "sisters", Francis also opened himself to that obscure part of himself which is rooted in nature; unconsciously he was fraternising with his own depths.'[5]

Thus reconciled with his own living powers, with his whole affective nature . . . man is born into a new personality, as large as the universe, open to the whole of being, welcoming to the mystery of the Other, in all its otherness. As brother of the sun and of all creation, Francis can go forward . . . free from all defensive reactions, all turning in on himself. In a violent world, bristling with castles, divided up by fortifications, as was that of the Middle Ages, his universe was without walls and fortresses. He was without frontiers.[6]

Here indeed is a restatement of that ancient vision of the interpenetration of man and the universe which is wonderfully expressed in the writings of the Fathers. 'Be on peaceful terms with thy soul; then heaven and earth will be on peaceful terms with thee. Be zealous to enter the treasury within; then thou wilt see that which is in heaven. For the former and the latter are one, and entering thou wilt see both. The ladder into the Kingdom is hidden within thy soul. Dive into thyself, freed from sin; there thou wilt find steps along which thou canst ascend.'[7] In England this same vision found a late but eloquent expression in the seventeenth century in the writings of Thomas Traherne.

You never enjoy the world aright, till the sea itself floweth in your veins, till you are clothed with the heavens and crowned with the stars; and perceive yourself to be the sole heir of the whole world: and more than so, because men are in it who are every one sole heirs, as well as you . . . till your spirit filleth the whole world, and the stars are your jewels, till you are familiar with the way of God in all ages as with your walk and table . . . till you delight in God for being good to all: you never enjoy the world.[8]

Here is a cosmic and personal vision of life and unity, a vision which answers in a curious way to one of the acutest problems of our own time, the problem of pollution and destruction of the environment. Very rapidly men are becoming aware that the lack of balance in their relationship with the material world around them arises from a lack of balance within themselves. The problem of pollution cannot be separated from the problem of inner alienation and disharmony, any more than it can be separated from the problem of harmony between men, the questions of social justice. All three dimensions of the questions – personal, social, cosmic – belong together, and though they may properly be distinguished they cannot be separated one from another.

Leclerc makes this point very forcefully when he comes to comment on the verse in the Canticle in praise of those who pardon and forgive. Though it is true that this verse was added after the composition of the main part of the song, he argues that it is by no means an accidental or merely occasional addition. Rather it reveals and completes the meaning of the whole. There is a profound link between 'the verses of cosmic praise, and the verse given over to pardon and peace'.[9] 'The Canticle is truly seen as the song of the man who is fully reconciled and at peace, in his relations with others, with himself.' It is to be understood not as a nostalgic longing for a lost paradise but as 'a vision of the world, dominated by the primacy of conciliation over discord, of unity over division . . . and this unity and this fullness are not to be sought by turning back to a primitive state of sleep, but through a deeper presence to oneself and to others'.[10] We cannot make a separation between our attitude towards people and our attitude towards things. 'The will towards reconciliation which inspires and characterizes all Francis's human relations goes closely together with his attitude of brotherliness, of a very deep, felt communion with the most humble elements of the cosmos.'[11] We cannot, whatever we may commonly think, 'combine an attitude of respect, welcome, and sympathy towards our fellow human beings, with an attitude of aggression, conquest and domination towards the whole of the rest of nature.'[12]

Thus Francis lived at one with all creation. His relations with the animals are perhaps the most widely remembered of all his characteristics, though not everyone remembers that he preached to fish as well as to birds, and would remove worms from the path so that they should not be trodden on. And here at once is one of the traits he shares in common with St Seraphim. In his years in the forest, St Seraphim lived very close to the animals, and had a particular friendship for the bears. Contrary to what is often said today, St Francis is not exceptional in his attitude towards the natural world, the animal kingdom. Rather, one might say, he gives an outstanding example of something which is seen in all the saints, but particularly in the saints of the Orthodox East. For in Orthodoxy this awareness of man's cosmic vocation has never been lost to sight, has never ceased to be an integral part of the vision of man's redemption.

As Vladimir Lossky puts it, in *The Mystical Theology of the Eastern Church*, resuming the teaching of St Maximus the Confessor, 'Man is not a being isolated from the rest of creation; by his very nature he is bound up with the whole of the universe . . . In his way to union with God, man in no way leaves creatures aside, but gathers together in his love the whole cosmos disordered by sin, that it may at last be transfigured by grace.'[13] To illustrate this point he quotes a remarkable passage from St Isaac the Syrian, a spiritual writer still highly commended in Orthodox monastic circles:

What is a charitable heart? It is a heart which is burning with love for the whole creation, for men, for the birds, for the beasts, for the demons — for all creatures. He who has such a heart cannot see or call to mind a creature without his eyes being filled with tears by reason of the immense compassion which seizes his heart; a heart which is softened and can no longer bear to see or learn from others of any suffering, even the smallest pain, being inflicted upon a creature. That is why such a man never ceases to pray also for the animals, for the enemies of truth, and for those who do him evil, that they may be preserved and purified. He will pray even for the reptiles, moved by the infinite pity which reigns in the hearts of those who are becoming united with God.[14]

There is no reason to suppose that St Francis and his first disciples were acquainted with the writings of St Isaac. But the description of the loving heart applies at once to the man of Assisi, whose companions report, 'We who were with him have seen him take inward and outward delight in almost every creature, and when he handled or looked at them his spirit seemed to

be in heaven rather than on earth.'[15] Nor is it likely that any
but the most indirect influence of the teaching of Maximus the
Confessor had reached thirteenth-century Italy. But we can hear
clearly the theme of what the Greek Fathers called *physike theoria*,
the contemplation of God in his creation, in this passage from the
first of Francis's biographers:

> He rejoiced in all the works of the hands of the Lord and saw
> behind all things pleasant to behold their life-giving reason and
> cause. In beautiful things he saw Beauty itself, all things were to
> him good. 'He Who made us is the best,' they cried out to him.
> Through his footprints impressed upon all things he followed the
> Beloved everywhere; he made for himself from all things a ladder
> by which to come even to his throne. He embraced all things with
> a rapture of unheard-of devotion, speaking to them of the Lord
> and admonishing them to praise him . . . He forbade the brothers
> to cut down the whole tree when they cut wood, so that it might
> have hope of sprouting again. He commanded the gardener to
> leave the border around the garden undug, so that in their proper
> times the greenness of the grass and the beauty of the flowers might
> announce the beauty of the Father of all things. He commanded
> that a little place be set aside in the garden for sweet-smelling
> flowering plants, so that they would bring those who looked upon
> them to the memory of the Eternal Sweetness. He removed from
> the road little worms, lest they be crushed under foot; and he
> ordered that honey and the best wines be set out for the bees,
> lest they perish from want in the cold of winter. He called all
> animals by the name 'brother', though among all kinds of animals
> he preferred the gentle. Who could possibly narrate everything?
> For that original goodness that will one day be all things and in
> all was already shown forth in this saint as all things in all.[16]

The terms of the final sentence in this passage need particularly
to be noted. That original goodness, that is to say, the creative
power of God who 'saw all that he had made and behold, it was
very good', will one day, in the end of all things, be all in all,
when things are gathered together in that final fulfilment which

the Gospel figures for us in the feast of the Kingdom. Even now that goodness which is declared in him who is the first and the last is communicated and made known in the persons of his saints, 'those who are becoming united with God'. One of the great images of this final blessedness is provided by the sun itself with its life-giving light and warmth. 'Then shall the righteous shine forth as the sun'; 'The sun of righteousness will arise, with healing in his wings.' Commenting on the primordial place amongst the creatures which the sun holds in St Francis's great Canticle, Leclerc speaks also of the inner sun, the great archetypal symbol of light which comes to life within him:

> Francis is clothed with the sun ... A symbol of the Most High, and yet a brother. A sun at once sacred and yet close to us. Francis does not simply see this sun, with his enfeebled eyes, shining over the plain of Assisi. He experiences it with all his being. The great cosmic image rises from the depths of his being. It is the expression of an inner fullness ... In it, Francis's soul recognises and celebrates symbolically, although unconsciously, his own transfiguration, his own transformation in the Kingdom ... This marvellous substance of the sun, all of light, so brotherly yet marked with the seal of the Most High, is the unconscious, but infinitely expressive image of the soul which finds itself in the fullness of its energies and destiny, open to the whole of its mystery, reconciling in itself the lower and hidden powers of life and matter, with the awareness of its highest destiny and the radiant certainty of its divine calling.[17]

It is impossible to read this passage without thinking at once of Motovilov's description of the transfiguration of St Seraphim (though Leclerc makes no mention of it). The saint is speaking:

> 'Why then, my friend, do you not look me straight in the face? Look freely and without fear; the Lord is with us.'
> Encouraged by these words, I looked and was seized by holy fear. Imagine in the middle of the sun, dazzling in the brilliance of its noontide rays, the face of the man who is speaking to you.

You can see the movements of his lips, the changing expression of his eyes, you can hear his voice, you can feel his hands holding you by the shoulders, but you can see neither his hands nor his body – nothing except the blaze of light which shines around, lighting up with its brilliance the snow-covered meadow, and the snowflakes which continue to fall unceasingly.

'What do you feel?' asked Father Seraphim.

'An immeasurable well-being,' I replied.

'But what sort of well-being? What exactly?'

'I feel,' I replied, 'such calm, such peace in my soul, that I can find no words to express it.'

'My friend, it is the peace our Lord spoke of when he said to his disciples: "My peace I give unto you", the peace which the world cannot give, "the peace which passes all understanding". What else do you feel?'

'Infinite joy in my heart.'

Father Seraphim continued: 'When the Spirit of God descends on a man, and envelops him in the fullness of his presence, the soul overflows with unspeakable joy, for the Holy Spirit fills everything he touches with joy . . .'[18]

Indeed, when the Holy Spirit touches the whole of a man, energizing and transforming his life at every level, a wonderful radiance of glory is released.

It has often been said, it is said by Lossky himself, that whereas the saints of the West are marked with the wounds of Christ, the saints of the East are transfigured with the divine light; whereas the one tradition concentrates its attention on the cross, the other lives in the light of the resurrection. Confronted with the figures of St Francis and St Seraphim, such a contrast seems superficial and oversimplified. What is evident in both is the manifestation of the joy and peace of the Kingdom through the way of the cross, which is known as the life-giving cross. What is evident in both is that at the end of their lives the light of God shines out through the very body of the one who has died with Christ so that he might live with Christ. In both traditions death and resurrection are inseparably linked together.

If we turn to the East, we find that the inner reality which the stigmata outwardly seal and express is by no means unknown in monastic tradition. The monk is one who can say in a particular way, 'I am crucified with Christ', one who bears 'in his body the marks of the Lord Jesus'. We can see this in more recent centuries in the frequently found icon which depicts the monk as fastened to the cross, subject to the attacks of the evil powers, identified with the Lord in his sufferings for man. We can see this at an earlier time by the way in which the calling of the pillar saints was understood. Their strange way of life was an extreme expression of the principle of monastic stability. In mounting the pillar, they were mounting the cross. We may remember even earlier the strange expressions in the Coptic life of St Pachomius which tell how a cherub appeared to him, took the measure of his chest, and 'crucified him on the earth', words which remind us directly of the story of St Francis.[19]

In the case of St Seraphim, the thousand days and nights which he spent standing on a rock in the forest, crying 'Lord have mercy', might be understood as his personal way of entering into this reality of the cross. The fifteen years which he spent in total seclusion in his cell, not even seeing the face of the brother who brought him his meals, would then correspond to the reality of being buried with Christ. We read of the radiance of the old man as he greeted everyone who came to him during the last years of his life with the salutation of Easter, 'My joy, Christ is risen.' We sometimes forget the long, hard years of silence and solitude and physical toil which preceded them. Before the resurrection had come the tomb.

On the other hand, when we turn to St Francis we find always that the love of the crucified Lord, and the pain and grief of the knowledge of his passion, is mingled with the joy and the peace which comes from the resurrection. In his prayer on Mount Alverna, on the very eve of the stigmata, Francis prays for two things, first that he may know as far as is possible in his own body the pain which our Lord suffered for all mankind, and secondly that he may know, as far as is possible, in his heart, the love which moved him to bear it. The radiance which had accompanied Francis in the first years of his conversion does not desert him in the last two years of his life. Quite the reverse; though broken in health, nearly blinded by the disease in his eyes, suffering from the wounds in his hands and feet and side, it is in this period that he writes the Canticle of the Creatures, and fills all who come to him with the awareness of the presence of the Kingdom.

For here, precisely, the two saints are at one in their anticipation – here and now – of the fullness of the end of all things. In the vision which came before the composition of the Canticle of the Creatures, Francis sees the earth, as it were, transmuted into gold, and receives the assurance that already he is in possession of a greater treasure in sharing in the joy of the Kingdom of Heaven. While at the very heart of the conversation of Father Seraphim with Motovilov lies the affirmation that already they are in the Holy Spirit, and the Holy Spirit is in them. 'For the heart of a man is capable of containing the Kingdom of God. The Holy Spirit and the Kingdom of God are one',[20] declares the saint. In both, the blessedness of the Kingdom is made known even in time. Through the brokenness of their bodies, the fullness and glory of the consummation of all things shines out.

St Benedict instructs us that the one who comes to enter the monastic brotherhood is to be asked 'whether he truly seeks God'. Here are two men who – following the way of the evangelical counsels – have not ceased to seek, and who have revealed in their lives something of that infinite capacity of the human heart for sorrow and for joy, for love and for understanding, which is made manifest if only we will give it up to God. Here are two men who reveal to us not only the deep underlying unity which joins together Churches canonically separated, but also the fact that such unity within the Church is inseparable from unity with all creation, and unity within the heart and mind of man. We need not fear, if we follow St Francis, that in estimating very highly the sacramental character of all created things, as he did, we shall undervalue the preciousness of the specific sacraments of the Church; on nothing does he insist more than on the honour which is due to the Eucharistic body of the Lord. But, again, in rating very highly the sacrament of the altar, we need not fear that we shall ignore the reality of the sacrament of our brother. The mysterious way in which the Lord comes to us in every man, and particularly in those who are despised and outcast, was experienced by Francis with an exceptional intensity. The social, personal, cosmic dimensions of reconciliation and unity are brought together in one.

And again, while we rightly celebrate the restoration of the monastic and religious order within our Church, we cannot but perceive in both St Francis and St Seraphim that the inner reality of the religious or monastic life overflows beyond the confines of the monastic institution. This surely is the meaning both of the calling of the Third Order, those who while living in the world are yet closely united in heart and mind with the Brothers and Sisters of the first two Orders, and of the way in which the First Order itself is sent out into the world. This surely also is part of the meaning of the fact that the conversation of St Seraphim is with a married layman, and that the saint assures him that their difference of outward status makes no difference to their common participation in the Kingdom of the Holy Trinity. Where the Spirit comes he brings unity, a unity which does not destroy but fulfils the diversity and richness of the world which God has made.

'The walls of separation do not reach up to heaven'; Metropolitan Platon of Kiev is evidently right. But, alas, they are still with us here on earth. The Churches to which St Francis and St Seraphim belonged have been out of communion with one another for nine hundred years. Over large areas and for long periods they have been divided by bitter hostility no less than by indifference and ignorance. Most of the faithful on either side of the divide are ignorant of the very existence of the saints of the other. Much of the official theology of both Greeks and Latins has denied the very possibility of holiness beyond the canonical boundaries of their Church. So strong has been the consciousness on both sides of the schism of the identity of the Church today with the Church before the schism, that in practice the existence of the other body as a real vehicle of God's saving power has been denied.

Nor should we as Anglicans congratulate ourselves over-much on our part in this tragic situation. Over long periods since the Reformation, and in some places still today, it is rare enough to

find any serious thought and concern about the restoration of
unity, or any living consciousness of the presence of the saints
with us, of their continuing intercession for us. We are, let us remember, a Church which is still not fully in communion with the
great apostolic sees either of East or West, nor fully recognized
by them. Nevertheless, in God's grace, the very fragility of our
position, the fact that we cannot be tempted to suppose that we are
the whole, gives us certain possibilities of openness to others which
we should use to the full. As we have thought at the beginning of
this essay, the movement which began in Oxford some one hundred and forty years ago involved not only a renewal of the sense
of catholicity within our own Church, but an affirmation of the
existence of an underlying unity between the separated branches
of the Christian family and of the reality of the communion of
saints across the barriers of death. The longing for unity which was
born then, and the renewed consciousness of our fellowship with
the saints, have not ceased to grow as the years have passed. We are
perhaps as a Church in a privileged position which enables us to
recognize not only privately but publicly the saints whom God has
given to other bodies, and even now to commemorate liturgically
the activity of the one Spirit, the presence of the one Lord,
amongst those with whom we are not in canonical communion.
In the various provinces of the Anglican Communion we have
growing opportunities for the commemoration of those who have
not previously been included in our official calendars. 'The walls
of separation do not reach up to heaven.' By the grace of God
they become less solid even here below.

There is then something that we can each of us do; not only in
prayer, though primarily there. Each one of us in some measure,
can make their own the words of Thomas Merton, 'If I can
unite *in myself* the thought and devotion of Eastern and Western
Christendom, the Greek and the Latin Fathers, the Russian with
the Spanish mystics, I can prepare in myself the reunion of divided
Christians. From that secret and unspoken unity in my self can
eventually come a visible and manifest unity of all Christians.'[21]
Each one of us can come, quite simply, to love and to know the
gifts of holiness which God has given to divided Christians even

in their state of separation, and can rejoice more fully in the activity of 'the divine grace which always fills up what is lacking and heals what is wounded'. We can, furthermore, take whatever opportunities are given us for making contacts across the barriers existing now; contacts not only of social courtesy and politeness, but contacts at the level of prayer and the sharing of spiritual gifts, seeking to understand more of the way in which the one Spirit has led us in the times of mutual estrangement. Here again there is much to be done, and much that communities, monastic and religious, are particularly capable of doing.

And all this will be of little avail unless it is rooted in a genuine growth in the love and knowledge of God. So that our work for Christian unity must be rooted in our prayer for the coming of the Holy Spirit, that he will descend upon the offering of the Church transmuting our gifts into his gift, that he will descend upon the offering which each one makes in the holy and most secret place of his own heart and mind. We must pray that we may have his gift of wisdom as well as his gift of praise, so that through us there may be a renewal of the theology of prayer. Above all, that in his coming, the reconciling presence of the Kingdom of the Father, the Son, and the Holy Spirit may be revealed amongst men, and all things hasten to their joyful consummation.

NOTES

1. The text of an address given at Tymawr Convent, Monmouthshire, to mark the sixtieth anniversary of the foundation of the Society of the Sacred Cross.

2. Quoted in M. Villain, *L'Abbé Paul Couturier, Apôtre de l'Unité Chrétienne* (Paris 1957), p.51.

3. St Stephen of Muret quoted in Rose Graham, *English Ecclesiastical Studies* (London 1929), p.212. I am grateful at this as at other points in this text to the suggestions of my friend, the Revd James Coutts.

4. T. Merton, *Contemplation in a World of Action*, p.211.

5. Eloi Leclerc, *Le Cantique des Créatures ou les Symboles de l'Union* (Paris 1970), p.200.

6. Ibid., p.201.

7. A.J. Wensinck, *Mystic Treatises of Isaac of Nineveh* (Wiesbaden 1969), p.8.

8. Thomas Traherne, *Poems, Centuries and Three Thanksgivings*, ed. Anne Ridler (London 1966), p.177.

9. Leclerc, op cit., p.202.

10. Ibid.

11. Ibid., p.197.

12. Ibid.

13. V. Lossky, *The Mystical Theology of the Eastern Church*, pp.110–11.

14. Ibid., p.111.

15. 'The Mirror of Perfection', 118, *S. Francis of Assisi. Writings and Early Biographies*, ed. M.A. Habig (Chicago   1972), p.1257.

16. II Celano, Cp. CXXIV, 165, *S. Francis of Assisi. Writings and Early Biographies*, pp.494–5.

17. Leclerc, op. cit., p.86.

18. Lossky, op. cit., pp.228–9.

19. See K.T. Ware in *Sacrament and Image*, edited by A.M. Allchin (London 1967), p.21.

20. St Seraphim of Sarov, quoted in Irina Gorainov, *The Message of Saint Seraphim* (SLG Press, Oxford 1973), p.14.

21. T. Merton, *Conjectures of a Guilty Bystander* (London 1966), p.12.

Canon A.M. Allchin is Director of the St Theosevia Centre for Christian Spirituality at Oxford, and has been Warden of the Sisters of the Love of God since 1967.

Affirming the Faith – in Singing

Dame Janet Baker Interviewed by The Revd John Barton

DAME JANET BAKER

J ohn Barton: Let us imagine a performance at Covent Garden. The house lights have dimmed, the conductor raises his baton, the audience is silent, the overture begins, and we, the audience, wait for the spectacle to begin. We, the audience, have paid for our tickets. What is the price, Dame Janet, that you have paid for being there?

Dame Janet: I think that's about the most interesting opening question I've ever been presented with. A very heavy price in terms of human qualities. People say, 'You can do it, you can get up there, you've been given the equipment.' Yes, absolutely true. The raw material, the voice, has been handed to me on a plate. So it is assumed automatically that because you can do something then everything should be straightforward and easy. I suppose the parish vicar is also in the same position. He has his tools of the trade, he can speak, he has his score, the most marvellous score, perhaps, of all time. But the problems start there, don't they? The problem of communication – and we're all in the business of communication – then begins.

The first price I have to pay is to remove myself from the scene of action, remove myself as a personality. Any communication, of course, must go through personalities. One is a human being talking or singing to other human beings, therefore the total removal of the human element is never possible. But the attempt of the communicator to be a medium is of paramount importance. One is communicating the composer's message to the audience, to the other side of the stage, but in doing so the communicator must get out of the way himself so that the music or the message can get through.

But the cost of the discipline you've had to use to develop your gift, the cost of being a public figure and having to be at your best night after night, what does this do to you as a person, physically, emotionally, mentally?

It has been a sort of agony for most of my working life; a pain, a torture, and a torment. I look back over the years and I wonder why I could not have come to where I am now, sooner. Why didn't I know, say, as a young performer in the chorus at Glyndebourne, the things I know now? But that is the question of everybody's life, one grows up too late. You become adult too late, but in a way it's not too late. I don't regret the years that I have suffered. Performing, for me at least, has been great suffering because I had not learned early enough what to do about it. All my life I have had the sense of having a vocation. I think and hope and believe that I have entered the profession for the right reasons, and the right reasons are for me to use what I've been given in God's service for the pleasure of other human beings. That has always been my guiding principle. But until very recently I have not connected that sense of vocation with what I now believe is a source of joy and pleasure and life enhancement for *myself*. I have felt music as a duty and the giving of my gift as a duty, and that's right. But in the process I'd forgotten that God gave this gift to *me*, first and foremost. He gave it to me. To discover a gift to oneself is like opening an unexpected Christmas present: 'How marvellous that this should be given to me!' – God's gift to me, to make me a whole and happy human being. To share that joy with other people is right and good, but I think I have been mistaken to think only of giving that joy to others. If I had grown up or grown into this feeling of the joy for myself first of all, then overflowing in that joy to other people, I might have spared myself some of the agony of forcing myself, all those years, to get up in a public place and perform. Performing might have been more of a joy for myself.

You have said that you loathe baring your soul in public. Is that because every role has to be played out with your own emotion or is there a kind of professionalism that enables you to just walk off the stage and say, 'Well, another job done'?

Not in my case. Being a professional singer doesn't give one leave to do that. I hope I am truly professional in the sense that when I am ill or I don't really want to go on I can still do so and maintain a certain standard. That is what one's training and one's intellectual disciplines provide. I believe I've always been able to do that. But for me, communication begins when one takes this step in faith and says to the audience in spirit, here am I as a performer. You're going to hear the composer's ideas through this human fallible machine. And in order to do that, I have to be as open and as honest as I possibly can. I have to try and get out of the way and be a transparency. But at the same time there has to be some extraordinary sort of soul-searching so that what I am giving people is basically honest, basically sincere, and is, in fact, using the raw material of my own emotional scene in order to float the composer's wishes on that. That is where the whole agony is. You stand in front of three thousand total strangers and say to them, well this is what you've got tonight. The music is coming through me. This is what I am and with all its faults and failings, this is the vehicle through whom you are going to get the music.

My struggle has been not to be able to allow myself to be a fallible human being. I've always wanted to be a perfect one. Where one falls in this terrible struggle to be a good vehicle, is in the knowledge that the preparation can never be good enough; you are always going to be fallible. As you get older, I think the ability to forgive yourself for being fallible becomes more possible. This is, I suppose, the fact and grace of growing into an adult human being – that you don't expect yourself to be perfect! But I wish that had happened in my life a little bit sooner.

But had you learned this earlier, without the long agony, would you have grown in the same way, achieved such greatness?

That's a very interesting question and I ask it of myself – would I? Perhaps the growing years have to be like this. One must not regret anything that happens to one as a human being, but use it and build upon it. Those years probably were necessary in my case because my attitude towards music and life in general has changed so much in the past two years since I stopped opera and that tremendous pressure has been removed. There are now wider gaps between the things that I do and my life is much more peaceful. I've begun to discover 'ordinary' life in a way that's never before been possible. One has always just gone from one thing to the next, always picking up a new score, always learning the new recital programme, going to a new place. The ordinary life – which to me is so extraordinary and so marvellous – is a new discovery. Had I been so interested earlier on in the wider interests I now have, perhaps I would not have been so concerned in serving the world musically. So I must not regret any of those years.

I remarked earlier that the audience had paid for their tickets. Do you feel that they have another responsibility, that they have an obligation beyond just sitting there? What to be an audience do we have to do?

First of all, I think an audience must *want* to be there. They must come to listen because they feel a need for music, for what music does to the heart and soul. You'd be surprised how many audiences feel quite differently. A lot of audiences come because it's the thing to do. [*We understand that, Dame Janet!*] So the first thing is to want to be there. Then, from the purely intellectual aspect of their own enjoyment, to have done a certain amount of homework beforehand. If you go to an opera that you don't know, for instance, you can't sit in front of a stage all night and expect to get quite a lot from a performance if you have done absolutely no advance work to prepare yourself for it. There are all kinds of things you can do. You can buy a score, you can play it through yourself, you can buy a record and listen to it. Some sort of background is necessary in order to make the experience of listening tremendously joyful and beneficial. Most of all, I think it is essential to forget any performance of the same work that you have perhaps heard before. One is so influenced by 'firsts' – the first time you see a Rembrandt, or the first time you see a Shakespeare play, or the first time you hear a Verdi opera. It's marvellous to remember and treasure such good moments, of course. They are going to colour your whole life. But if they colour your judgement so that each time you see the same Verdi opera or you listen to the Matthew Passion you think, well, it's not what it was ten years ago, then you are not seeing and hearing what is happening *now*.

Music for me is *now*. Records have a marvellous place in the world – and books. We couldn't do without any of these things. But the whole point of what I call communication is the *moment*. When that moment is coloured by former impressions or judgements, these things can be a screen and they can stop what is happening now from doing its work on the person now. And that, I feel, is very sad. We want open minds and a clear passageway between the communicator and those communicated with. It must be at the moment.

So the artist has done her preparation, the audience some homework. Is it just a matter of keeping those rules or is this moment of 'now' something mysterious as well?

Very much so. All this is only groundwork. There is no such thing as a perfect performance or a perfect performer, and the moments that transcend all the basic work and preparation are indescribable. They are magic moments that we all hope for, but they are entirely out of everybody's control.

Question from audience: *Would you say that composers have to suffer in order to produce great music?*

This brings up the question of human suffering, doesn't it? What is suffering for one person is not for another. We're talking about a basic human condition. We all have our own sufferings, but mine may not be yours. We each have to tackle our own area. Of course great people suffer. I think composers, creative people, are in a particularly vulnerable position because they have to be more open to, more sensitive to, more aware of the emotional area in any kind of creative work than the rest of us. I would think that what makes a creative person suffer would be almost any moment of life, which might not affect the rest of us in quite the same way. Because they *are* vulnerable, their lives must be full of suffering in ways that are painful to them. All our lives are like this. We all have to suffer in our own way: unfortunately, in my case, the things I learned seemed to come from the kick in the pants, not from the glorious moments – they seemed always to be from the hard bits! And the really creative people, those who produce something out of nothing, as opposed to the re-creative, which is my field, perhaps suffer especially. Those I've been privileged to know have been terribly vulnerable, and their path through life has been a very hard one. So, I suppose the greater you are, the greater your capacity for creativeness and sensitivity, so too is your capacity to suffer, really.

Question from audience: *You've given many of us great joy for many years; what work, to sing, has given you the greatest joy, and why?*

Again it's a question of association. Church music. I was brought up with church music; my first music was singing in the choir. Fischer-Dieskau was telling me that his experience was exactly the same. His first memories of music are of church music. For me, the great moments in music are in religious music, and my whole being responds then in a way that is different. It has an extra dimension. So I would say that the work that means the most to me as a total person is the St Matthew Passion. For me it expresses the total value of what I mean by being a musician. But I must also say that any piece of music I have to sing also has a feeling of sacredness about it, because I am expressing very deep human emotions and there is something sacred about those emotions too. Even in a completely secular work, you are still a human being, expressing human emotions to others, and you can't divide that from the holy either. But I couldn't live without the St Matthew Passion.

Question from audience: *It's been marvellous to associate you with the Elgar Anniversary celebrations. Some of us will have seen your television performance of Gerontius at the Three Choirs Festival. I wonder how*

much singing that particular work is a spiritual experience, how much
you are caught up in the experience of performing – or is it a case of while
all around are losing their heads, you've got to keep yours?

Gerontius is a particularly dear work to me because, like the St
Matthew Passion, it is a total expression of what I believe music
and life is about. I've sung it so much, yet when I get up there, it
is as though I haven't performed the work before. The Worcester
performance recently was a tremendous case in point. I stood up
in Worcester Cathedral that night and suddenly realized that I
had changed since the last time I had sung the piece. I had
learnt things; I had discovered things; I had lived a bit more.
In a way it was as if I had never sung the work before. The
building, of course, is also a tremendous factor. Singing religious
music in a church, or any music in a church, is very special for
me because the building, like the people, speaks to me and adds
something indefinable but very real. I try to keep myself open to
this feeling as well as to what I have learnt between performances.
Something always comes to me, something I understand that I
hadn't understood before – and it certainly did that night. The
act of communication itself teaches me.

In a performance I am totally concentrated but there is an
area which is also standing aside and watching. I am deeply
involved emotionally, of course. When I am studying a work
at home I often get completely overcome by the emotions of,
say, a Schubert song, or something I am reworking at the piano,
and I start to cry. Then I think, well that's fine; I have to feel
deeply about it. Good! I'm not blasé about this piece yet. I can
still perform it in public because I can still feel very deeply about
it. Now, if I were to stand up to perform at a moment like that
and begin to cry, I would not be able to sing because the crying
uses the equipment I need to be able to speak or sing. I am
useless as a communicator if my equipment is faulty because of
emotional upheaval. My own private emotional upheaval has to be
there at some point, but then it sinks to a deeper level, somehow.
And when I'm serving the score, this quality of balance or poise or
equilibrium must have the upper hand so that you, the audience,

will share in what I feel at this deep level without me being a shield because I am overcome by emotion.

In your book [Full Circle, Penguin Books, 1984] you said that public adulation or the critics do not mean very much to you, but that the concern and appreciation of fellow artists matters enormously . . . I wonder if the special relationship with those you work with is something akin to what in the church we would call communion with others, or fellowship?

I think that is absolutely true. One's colleagues are a group of people with the same ideal, we are fellow servants trying to create a standard of something. We are all working towards the same point . . . Also the fact that others in my profession know what I am and what I believe, what I take into my work situation, is important. As a senior member of the profession, my behaviour, my ideas, the way I react to other people, everything about me is closely observed. I feel it is terribly important, especially when young people are about, to show them (if I can) that a soloist has responsibilities of a very particular kind not only towards the music, but towards a group of people. If I don't behave in what I consider to be the proper way, then people will think, 'Well, that's licence to kill! This is how prima donnas behave.'

The general idea of a prima donna is most extraordinary! Most prima donnas are not at all like what one reads in magazines and the press. Once you enter the arena, you have to be responsible in every possible way, and I've always felt that to be a particular joy, actually. Of course, I can be as temperamental as the next, I hope for the right reasons, particularly when people are not doing their jobs!! I get very angry and it's not a pretty thing to see. I admit it, I'm not ashamed of it. But I do hope my colleagues know that I try to behave responsibly towards them.

Music has been your life; books have been a passion. Which books? What do you read?

I read ideas. The world of ideas to me has been my saving grace. First of all, the tradition, the church tradition in which I've been brought up. I can't begin to thank my parents enough for giving me, as a child, the particular structure on which to build my life. When I left home at the age of twenty that was the only thing I had to lean on, and by golly I leant on it! I'll never forget those years when my faith was really tested to a tremendous extent. The commitment I made to my profession was a direct result of that, and the hardships and poverty as a student would not have been bearable had there not been a more important reason than a career. Therefore, I have all these years been reading things that develop my faith. I am a Christian. I am trying to be a Christian with all that that involves. What that involves for me at this moment, and has all my life, is a discovery of what other people are believing and thinking: what makes their faith and their belief work for them, and how I can share in that, or how I can explore those avenues in order to strengthen my own belief.

Question from audience: *Your interest in comparative religion has taken you into a meditation group. Can you tell us about that?*

Yes, I can. I think this is probably the most important and fascinating aspect of my life at this moment. My mother died seven years ago and that was a very deeply traumatic and painful event. I don't believe that a life lived with any grain of faith is accidental. I believe every step of my own way has been in some sense guided, and seven years ago I met, I was introduced to, a number of people. Everything that I'd read on my own, on journeys all those years, had been a discovery of my own. I would sit in a church alone, say, at Easter in Chicago, and my whole experience of discovery in the faith was alone. Then suddenly at this moment in my life another door opened for me. I began to discover people with whom I could talk about the most deeply important things which I'd always kept inside. This was a tremendous moment in my life – that I could actually share with strangers a depth of communication which up till then had not been possible. The group I was introduced to (I suppose it would be labelled 'Sufi', although there are no labels for this sort of exploration) is a group of people who meet once or twice a week for what might be described as silent prayer.

We meet in a house in North London, and we 'sit'. I suppose we all think about different things. I don't know what anybody else thinks about in meditation, it's a very special area, we all have our own ways of meditating. Mine is a Christian meditation. My dialogue is with the Christ symbol, the Christ figure which, through meditation, has become not just an outside figure but an inner one. I am beginning to join things up in a way that hadn't been possible before, and the very exciting thing is that I'm finding for the first time in my life that I can communicate with people not only as a musician, which is the only avenue I had ever thought I would be able to share, but in every aspect of ordinary everyday life as well. My religion is expressed not only in my professional commitment but in the whole of my life. I am beginning to discover that religion, one's Christian life, is a moment-by-moment experience: the meditation aspect of it I would describe as having a relationship with Christ within, in silence and in listening. Then when that moment of contemplation is over, you go out into the world again which is also a meditative and religious experience. Like night and day these moments belong together: one is like an indrawn breath, and the other is like an exhalation. Different areas of my life are beginning to join up and make a whole, which again is a remarkable moment-by-moment discovery. Miraculous!

How much has Jung influenced you?

I read Jung many years ago and still do in an attempt to find an answer to what to do about the ten feet that separate the outside world from the centre of the platform. How to walk those ten steps from the green-room, how to survive that, and how to stand on the stage and function. We're all nervous, but my fear was something much more than that. Standing in the green-room, all dressed up like a dog's breakfast, I'd ask myself in agony, 'What am I doing here, suffering like this, surely life isn't meant to be like this?' I read Jung in an attempt to find an answer to this terrible, terrible struggle that was going on in me. Maybe it's not possible to be without it if you have something to give. I don't have the answer. Jung didn't have it either!

I mentioned Jung because I thought he might be your great apostle of human internal integration. But clearly for you it's been more a matter of meditation and relationship with God through Christ.

Yes. Everything seems to lead me back there, perhaps because I was brought up as a Christian. I suppose a committed Buddhist would say the same for his faith. With all my reading, with all my exploration, I am brought back to the figure of Christ. He is the solid basis on which I was reared and I cannot turn my back on that. And I don't need to. Whenever I have discovered something outside our own particular square box, I find that what is in the box is somehow illumined; it's there in a different way, perhaps, but the truth is still there.

You strongly believe in God's providence guiding you each moment. Have you also got a strong doctrine of rewards and punishments – that you get out of life what you put into it?

It's probably one of my difficulties, to think that if I am 'good', I shall be a good singer, or if I do 'this' I shall give a good performance. It doesn't work out that way. I've really been up a gum tree there! I'm not so concerned now with rewards and punishments. I am much more ready to think of myself both as a fallible human being and as a fallible musician. This is a very difficult thing to accept because one wants so badly to give the composer one's all. Well, my all includes the fear and the nerves – everything. I have to accept that and I'm beginning to do so.

What is emerging and is so marvellous is the feeling of being wholly loved. I suppose when I lost my mother I lost that feeling. I have marvellous other loves – my husband, my father, very special friends – so I'm not short of love by any means. My mother's love was always very important to me and it was removed, so I suppose I was searching for a substitute. Now I'm beginning to realize there is no love in the outside world which can provide you with the sense of being totally loved except the Christ love. There is no other base on which you can walk forward into the dark. But it's a relatively new thing to discover this divine love

within, love which sees you at every moment, every second of
the day, and which accepts you as you are. I now have so much
more confidence in myself as a person and as a performer because
I feel totally loved within. And because I am beginning to learn
to love myself as I am, I hope very much I am beginning to love
my neighbour. I think, for me, it has to work in that direction.

Question from audience: *It's quite clear that your main aim when
singing, is to give your audience enjoyment. Could you define enjoyment
in singing terms?*

Enjoyment for me means the absence of the agony, the absence
of self-judgement beyond a certain point. I know when I sing
well and when I don't. I know when my voice is behaving
right as a mechanical box. As I grow older, I have less control
over that. My body is asserting its own authority and I have
to come to terms with that. It's not very enjoyable on days
when the voice is not working as perfectly as I think it should.
So the fact that my instrument is working well is a source of joy
to me.

  As I said at the start, I've so wanted other people to enjoy
my God-given gift that I've not been sharing in it myself. It was
a revelation when a friend pointed out that the gift is given to
me to enjoy first of all. And as I use it, I feel it is a grace, and a
healing, and a wholing process. The marvellous thing about life
now is that I *am* sharing the enjoyment. I'm no longer afraid
to be myself out there; and this is so world-shattering to me,
compared to the way I felt before, that it affects every area of
my life. So my enjoyment, my joy is in this absence of fear. I
love it when people enjoy what I'm doing but that's not really
my concern. The real joy is in the absence of things which stop
the music from flowing through me.

Dame Janet Baker gave this interview during the Canterbury Diocesan
Conference at the University of Sussex in September 1984.

The Poetry of Vision, the Prose of Trials

The Dark Nights of St John of the Cross

SISTER EILEEN MARY SLG

As John of the Cross lay dying in the Carmelite Friary of Ubeda four hundred years ago, on 7 December 1591, he asked for verses from the Song of Songs to be read to him. As he listened he was heard to murmur, *'O que preciosas margaritas!'* – 'What precious pearls.' As in life, so in death this Old Testament poem was the spiritual food which sustained him as he passed from this world to the next. The quality of love which he found there forms the background of all John's teaching on the Dark Night of the soul. Despite the darkness, fear, and seeming abandonment, love is God's meaning. Darkness and light are held together within the glorious mystery of the otherness of God who can only reveal himself to us in the measure in which we try to accept him as he is. For we are often only interested in a God who will assuage our hopes and calm our fears. But these things can only happen as the centre of our lives moves away from ourselves to him. Within the emptiness and silence of the Dark Night we sense the reality behind the self-created images.

So John is not concerned with satisfying wishful thinking:

> . . . we are not writing on pleasing and delightful themes addressed to the kind of spiritual people who like to approach God along sweet and satisfying paths.
>
> (Prologue to *The Ascent of Mount Carmel*, 8)

His appeal is to the young in heart of every age who will persevere in seeking God in the darkness, rather than in spite of it.

> O night more lovely than the dawn!
> O night that has united
> The Lover with His beloved,
> Transforming the beloved in her Lover.
>
> (*Dark Night*, 5)

However, John does not underestimate the pain and bewilderment that the soul will experience:

> Where have You hidden,
> Beloved, and left me moaning? . . .
> I went out calling You, and You were gone.
>
> (*Spiritual Canticle*, 1)

The way is one of love and trust rather than of intellectual understanding which soon finds itself out of its depth:

> The higher he ascends
> The less he understands,
> Because the cloud is dark
> Which lit up the night.
>
> (*I Entered Into Unknowing*, 5)

The capacity to love God is infused into the heart of every Christian, although we may sometimes find this difficult to believe in our own case! For though John's teaching is expressed in the technical language of scholastic theology, he himself relied rather on the heart than on the head. So he explains to Mother Anne of Jesus, to whom he dedicated his *Spiritual Canticle*,

> Even though Your Reverence lacks training in scholastic theology by which the divine truths are understood, you are not wanting in mystical theology which is known through love and by which one not only knows but at the same time experiences.
>
> (Prologue to *The Spiritual Canticle*, 3)

'Mystical theology' is not something élitist or esoteric. It is that core of faith which maintains a personal relationship with God even when he is experienced as felt absence rather than felt presence.

The Dark Nights and the Soul

John's poetry of the Dark Night was in no way sentimental, for it sprang from a life which was always hard and sometimes terrifying. Even as he lay peacefully dying with the words of the Song of Songs on his lips, his material situation was far from ideal. Apart from the physical pain of his last illness, he had not been made welcome in the Friary to which he had come for medical treatment. The Inquisition was plotting against him and, had he survived, his works could have been destroyed and he himself imprisoned, or worse. Like John, we need the poetry of vision and the prose of trials to be held together if our Christian life is to be real and wholesome.

We do not have to abandon the insights of the twentieth century for John's teaching to be helpful for us today. But we do need to enter with imagination and sympathy into his world during the time that we are studying his writings. Otherwise we shall not be able to discern and use what is applicable to us in the context of our own society. John's teaching on the Dark Nights is based on a particular theory about the make-up of the human person. It is of his time, but this does not invalidate the truth of his doctrine for us today. The human components of which he speaks are in us too, even though we can no longer discuss them in separate compartments as he did. Even so, John is well aware that the spirit affects the senses and vice versa, although he only describes one aspect at a time.

For John the Dark Nights do their work in and through a human body which contains a sensual-soul and a spiritual-soul. We share the former with the animal world, for in common with animals we possess the senses of sight, hearing, touch, taste and smell, together with memories of past pleasure or pain associated with them. These are wonderful gifts through which we relate to the outside world, but they readily condition us into believing that their satisfaction is the prime object of life. In the Active and Passive Nights of Sense we become de-conditioned; we find ourselves capable of using or not using our senses freely, as God and a particular situation seem to require.

Unlike the animals, human beings have within them a spiritual-soul which is capable of more complex powers of understanding, memory and will. Joy, sorrow, fear and hope are centred around more permanent and solid loves which often have great value in themselves. We may think, for example, of the potency of nationalism, religious culture, love of family or of a particular work for God. It is because of their innate goodness that they can so easily escape out of the hierarchy of love to become lesser gods themselves. Therefore the spiritual-soul too needs its Active and Passive Nights, whereby these loves are restored to their rightful place within the all-embracing love of God. At the top of the map of Mount Carmel which precedes Book I of *The Ascent*, we find written, 'Only the honour and glory of God dwell on this Mount'.

John does not deny the reality of the deprivation involved, but if we want the freedom of the children of God there is a price to be paid. In his opinion, the rewards are so great and the cost so small in comparison that he is amazed at the fuss that we tend to make about suffering:

> How amazing and pitiful it is that ... the hand of God, though light and gentle, should feel so heavy and contrary. For the hand of God does not press down or weigh upon the soul, but only touches it; and that mercifully, for God's aim is to grant it favours and not chastise it.
>
> *(Dark Night*, II, v, 7)

We may need to remind ourselves of this when we read John's writings, for at first sight we may feel that there is little positive doctrine of creation to be found there. We may be repelled by passages which seem to deny the goodness of created things and even of human love. Yet whenever we find an apparent negative in John's work, we need to look behind it to the positive which balances it. In his own life there was ample evidence of love for the natural world, for the brethren of his Order, and for his own natural family. But there is a right hierarchy of love, and when this is set in place we are free to love whom and what we will:

> God gathers together all the strength, faculties, and appetites of the soul, spiritual and sensory alike, that the energy and power of this whole harmonious composite may be employed in this love. The soul consequently arrives at the true fulfilment of the first commandment which, *neither disdaining anything human nor excluding it from this love*, states: 'You shall love your God with your whole heart and with your whole mind and with your whole soul and with all your strength'.
>
> (*Dark Night*, II, xi, 4)

This is a Gospel affirmation which Christians of any century can accept.

The Active Night of Sense

We experience the Night throughout our Christian lives, but as John points out in *The Ascent* II, i and ii, the quality and depth of its darkness varies. The pilgrim sets out in the twilight of the Nights of Sense, in which he or she has at least some idea of what is being asked and what is being given. The keynote of the Active Night of Sense is given in *The Ascent* I, xiii, 3 and 4:

> First, have a habitual desire to imitate Christ in all your deeds by bringing your life into conformity with His. You must then study His life in order to know how to imitate Him and behave in all events as He would.
>
> Second, in order to be successful in this imitation, renounce and remain empty of any sensory satisfaction that is not purely for the honour and glory of God. Do this out of love for Jesus Christ. In His life He had no other gratification, nor

desired any other, than the fulfilment of His Father's will,
which He called His meat and food. (John 4:34)

This advice may sound over-simplistic to us today. Our purity
of heart will probably lie in the perseverance by which we go on
trying and the readiness with which we return to God after any
falling-away.

The type of prayer which John is describing is associated with
St Ignatius Loyola and involves the active use of the imagination
and senses:

> A person in this state should be given matter for meditation and
> discursive reflection, and he should by himself make interior acts
> and profit in spiritual things from the delight and satisfaction of
> the senses.
>
> (*Living Flame of Love*, Stanza III, 32)

Through this interest and delight, John hopes that the soul
will become attached to the things of God and therefore less
conditioned by the things of this world. Nowadays the essence
of this form of meditation may have been acquired in less formal
ways. We may have absorbed it through our Christian education,
even through work done for examinations, through spiritual
reading of the Bible, and through literature, plays or films. The
one essential is that Jesus becomes for us a living person for whom
we are prepared to sacrifice our lesser gods if necessary. For we
want to become like the one we love.

This will inevitably involve some measure of darkness, pain
and irritation, as props which may seem harmless need to be
abandoned, at least for a time, because we are hooked on them.
So there is no cast-iron rule about what needs to be set aside.
What is harmful for me may not be so for you. In *The Ascent*
I, xiii, 6, John gives a set of recommendations which may repel
modern readers if they are not understood aright:

> Endeavour to be inclined always:
>
>> not to the easiest, but to the most difficult;
>>
>> not to the most delightful, but to the harshest;

> not to the most gratifying, but to the less pleasant;
> not to what means rest for you, but to hard work . . .

So the passage continues in the same vein until we wonder
what kind of God it is who seems to be interested only in our
misery! This is not so. But in the Active Night of Sense he
makes us aware of a potential within us which we have not
used and on a natural level are too fearful or lazy or sceptical
to stimulate. We are asked only to *endeavour* to give a priority to
those things that we dislike, for those that we prefer are already
over-catered for. If we do this we may find that after a period
of constriction, and maybe depression, our horizons will have
widened and our values changed. But this can only happen if
we are inspired by love of the God who made and redeemed us
and love for a self that is so much greater than we realize. Grim
stoicism will accomplish nothing. We need to allow ourselves to
listen to the messages that our senses send us, even though our
answer to them need not necessarily be 'Yes'.

Myths and fairy tales endure because they say something true
about our human condition. One such story is that of Beauty and
the Beast. In the eyes of young love, the Beast may represent all that
is strange, difficult, humiliating and undesirable. Beauty has the
attractiveness of youth, but her judgements are narrow and shallow
and her ability to love is small. It is only as she brings herself to
embrace the Beast that he shows himself in his true light as the
prince of her dreams. In union with him her horizons widen, her
values change and she becomes more lovable herself. Christ often
comes to us in forms which we do not recognize or desire. Only
as we embrace this Stranger do we come to find delight and con-
solation in what he represents. For we ourselves are changing.

The Passive Night of Sense

Active meditation based on the many different methods available
to us today may have brought us to a place of comparative inner
peace and order. On the other hand, we may flit from one method
to another as each in turn brings us to the full stop which marks

the beginning of the Passive Night of Sense. Most people, John says, who practise mental prayer come to this point quite soon. It marks the beginning of a different, more direct, relationship with God which at first may cause distress, scruples and a sense of boredom, as the ability to meditate is taken from us. We are left in a 'blank' in which nothing seems to live or move. In prayer we are capable only of the few words of hope and longing addressed to a God whom we cannot see. Yet in the end, if we persist, there is a stirring within the darkness, revealing a Presence and a strength more real and desirable than anything conveyed through the medium of the senses. This Night is called passive because we are called into it by God. It is not the result of self-hypnosis. The darkness is deeper and we no longer see objects around us, nor know and direct our own path.

In *The Ascent*, II, xiii, and in *The Dark Night*, I, ix, John gives three signs which need to be present together if the call to change our mode of prayer is a genuine one. First there is the inability to meditate, however hard we try; secondly, although we cannot sense God's presence, nothing else will do in his place; and thirdly, there needs to be some ability to stay quiet and still in God's presence with no particular image of him. This stillness of the heart does not exclude a riot of thoughts which may churn around in our heads. It only means that we pay no attention to them, returning again and again to the still centre of being within us, even if it be twenty times in ten minutes.

Looking back, I believe that the process of life brings us into this Night, even though we may be beginners on the spiritual way. It is not possible to meditate in an air raid shelter waiting for the next bomb to fall, nor during a period of severe illness, nor in one of the devastating blows or disappointments that life may bring us. We may be too confused and tense for active thought, but nevertheless we have an aching need for God. So we are drawn through necessity to seek him within, finding there a point of life from which we can draw strength. Once found, the prayer deepens with use and we no longer want nor expect sensual recompense from it.

The Active Night of Spirit

Now, in terms of darkness, twilight is deepening into a Night in which the ways of logical reason will be replaced by other modes of seeing and responding. John calls this the Active Night of Spirit, in which most maturing Christians spend much of their lives. In the alternation between activity and passivity God teaches us in two different ways. In the passive states we experience his omnipotence working in our life and prayer. Our only resource lies in his wisdom and mercy. But in the Active Nights we are co-creators with him. We recognize the wonderful powers of heart, mind and spirit which are given to us as human beings and understand that God is asking us to use them in the working out of our salvation and transformation. When we read of the courage and love of hostages and their families, the resilience of children suffering from terrible diseases; when we see the power of non-violence at work, then we know that human beings are capable of far more than they realize. John tells us that in the Active Night of Spirit a profound change may take place through the practice of faith, hope and charity. In everyday situations the way in which our minds work will be altered if decisions and judgements are consciously made on the basis of faith. This will not negate our critical faculty, but it will free our minds from dependence on our own narrow outlook. There will be room for the Holy Spirit to operate in and through us. Our memory, at once a treasure house and dustbin, will make its selections in accordance with trust and hope in God's guidance and love. This will counteract the depression and self-doubt with which so many of us are afflicted. Such choices are not hypocritical, for we are affirming a truth which for us lies in the future, not claiming that it is a present reality. And if our wills consciously try to act in charity we may hope to increase our capacity to love and understand others and ourselves.

To grow in these things requires hard work which does not always seem either sensible or just. Life is not fair, people manipulate us and we feel that they deserve rebuke rather than understanding. Perhaps they do, but John tells us that right judgement depends on our recognition of the often unconscious passions which move us, even when we think that we are being most objective. In our complicated lives, joy, hope, grief, and sorrow are centred around many objects besides the love and honour of God. For instance we may find joy and reliance in worldly possessions, or natural gifts and sensitivities or in our own moral rectitude. We may give too much weight to any supernatural, charismatic or spiritual gifts that we possess. Many of these are good and centred around worthy objects, but nevertheless they can become little gods if God is not first in our lives.

The Active Night of Spirit asks for small, continuous responses of faith, hope and charity when our unredeemed selves would prefer to act very differently. We plod through the Night, a step at a time, but nevertheless are travelling in the right direction. A born-again Christian of twenty years' standing was asked what those years had been like. He admitted that in some ways they had been quite awful, what with himself, other people and the Church. Then why, the interviewer asked, had he persevered? 'Because I know that God loves me and that I can be used by him,' was the reply. That is the ultimate Christian answer.

The Passive Night of Spirit

All along our path God will have been giving us glimpses of the daybreak in order to encourage us to persevere. Gradually the light may seem steadier and more penetrating. Yet between ourselves and our entering-in may lie the deeper darkness which John calls the Passive Night of Spirit. He describes this vividly in his well-known image of the log and the fire. God works upon the soul just as the fire burns up the log. In common with the log, human beings are made of good material, capable of being transformed if they remain in the fire (or on the Cross as Jesus chose to do). We experience the action of the fire upon deep instincts, fears and desires which we hardly knew we possessed. In fact, all that is foreign to our true humanity is being dried out and the rest will be transformed in the flames. We fear that it is the essence of ourselves which is being destroyed in ashes and ruin, but in actual fact, as John says, we are no worse than we ever were. Now, meeting no resistance, the fire transforms the wood into its own life:

> Once transformed, the wood no longer has any activity or passivity of its own, except for its weight and its quantity which is denser than the fire. For it possesses properties and performs the actions of fire: it is dry and it dries; it is hot and it gives off heat; it is brilliant and it illumines; and it is also light, much lighter than before. It is the fire that produces all these properties in the wood.
>
> (*Dark Night*, II, x, 1)

What John is describing is real, inescapable suffering, not something invented or built up by ourselves. Its context may be commonplace; a marriage, our family, our work, a prolonged illness. Many of us will know the tedious frustrations and deprivations of old age. As we go on living as positively as we can, we may not even realize that we are in this Night until a sudden ray of light shows us something of its value and meaning. John tells us that though the intensity of suffering is only felt at intervals, the Night itself may last for some years if it is to do its work of purification properly. But God does not want or like our suffering. Sado-masochism is our invention, not his. John says that the work will go on just as long as it is necessary if we are to become 'one with the Spirit of God, according to the degree of union of love that God, in His mercy, desires to grant' (*Dark Night*, II, vii, 3). Our faith now rests in God's contemplation of us rather than our contemplation of him. We believe that we are the subject of his prayer and work and affirm this even in the midst of our darkness. Faith is the umbilical cord that unites us to him.

I believe that it is this factor which goes far to differentiate the Passive Night of Spirit from psychological depression. For it is true that some of the symptoms may be similar. Yet if there is the faintest touch of love in us we may find within our dreadful isolations some sense of union with the world's darkness and a power which is not our own. Our place is to stay with the situation, hoping against hope:

... in the midst of these dark and loving afflictions, the soul feels the presence of someone and an interior strength which so fortifies and accompanies it that when this weight of anxious darkness passes, it often feels alone, empty, and weak.

(Dark Night, II, xi, 7)

The power of God is within the pressure, not in spite of it. Non-violence towards ourselves is advisable in the Passive Night of Spirit. Our darkness may well be due to physical or emotional damage in our past or present, but even if we are at fault we do better to nurse rather than curse ourselves. Any small act of faith, hope and charity, made perhaps with infinite difficulty, will help to hold us to life.

Desolation, anguish, a sense of helplessness, are not morbid when they are appropriate to a given situation. We may think that the depth of agony described in Chapters v to viii of Book II of *The Dark Night* must be exaggerated, but read in the light of John's experiences in his Toledo prison this is not so. It would have been more abnormal had he not let himself feel the pain.

John tells us that all darkness contains the seeds of joy within it if it is accepted and carried in the spirit of the Cross. Christ's Cross was a passage, not an end in itself, and led to the bursting open of the narrowness of human limitation in resurrection-life. We cannot know exactly what this means for us, but John tells us that it is the path by which we return to the wholeness which God intended for the human race when he created it at the beginning. Our destiny is to be scarcely less than divine with the individual soul 'being united to and absorbed in Him, as it is in this state' *(Living Flame of Love, Stanza 2, 34)*.

John has associated the various states of Night with different stages of discipleship, but in actual experience we find that there is no hard and fast rule. There will never be a time when we shall not need to practise the disciplines of the Active Nights in some form. But as we get older we may no longer see them as a trial but as a support and stay for sagging bodies and spirits; whereas, in the insecurity of today's world many young people may experience something of the desolation of the Passive Nights even if they would not recognize them by that name.

Our Nights are the small portion of Christ's Cross which he gives us to share with him. It is a work, and indeed feels like it; Christ's greatest work was his death:

> And by it He accomplished the most marvellous work of His whole life . . . That is, He brought about the reconciliation and union of the human race with God through grace.
>
> (*Ascent* II, vii, 11)

It does not matter what our individual vocation in the Church and world may be; this is our universal priesthood. We do not have to wait to exercise it until our feeble love has taken on something of the quality of Trinitarian love. Every stumbling effort on our part is for everyone else. Our right concern for ourselves and our own healing and wholeness is a part of a whole in which there need be no conflict or separation of interest.

The Night purifies our outward activity and service, giving it a mysterious otherness which is prayer, even though we may have little time for saying prayers. And when for one reason or another we are withdrawn from active life, our essential priesthood remains.

> Now I occupy my soul
> And all my energy in His service;
> I no longer tend the herd,
> Nor have I any other work
> Now that my every act is love.
>
> (*Spiritual Canticle*, Stanza 28)

Priesthood involves both sacerdotal offering at the altar and pastoral service. Most of us have a herd to tend for much of our lives, and it is right that it should be so. But until death and beyond there is never a time when we cannot offer the oblation of ourselves on the altar of our love. It is the one human activity in which we can embrace everybody all the time, and so our sacrifice and our pastoral service become one.

Sister Eileen Mary entered SLG in 1952, and is at present living at Bede House, Kent. From 1983 to 1987 she was seconded to the Columbanus Community of Reconciliation, Belfast, as a foundation member of that interchurch community.

The Mystery of Love in Solzhenitsyn

A Conference given to the Novitiate on the Vow of Chastity

SISTER EDNA MONICA SLG

I wonder how many people read footnotes! It was in a footnote to the second volume of Solzhenitsyn's *Gulag Archipelago* that I found confirmed my intuition that his writings had great relevance to the monastic life. Solzhenitsyn describes the Solovetsky Islands, rising in their paradisiacal beauty from the White Sea, having several hundred lakes replete with fish, their lands full of grouse, hare and deer, while no beasts of prey have ever appeared there. 'Half a thousand years before the GPU' (human beasts of prey?), two monks crossed the sea in a tiny boat and the Solovetsky Monastery came into being with them. 'In all this brightness it is as if there were no sin present . . . It is as if nature had not yet matured to the point of sin,' is the Russian writer Prishvin's perception. But in 1923 the monks were all thrown out and the northern Special Purpose camps were concentrated on the Solovetsky Islands, partly housed in the monastic buildings. Solzhenitsyn comments on his quotation from Prishvin in the footnote:

And to Prishvin only the monks themselves seemed sinful in the context of Solovki. It was 1908, and in accordance with the liberal concepts of the times it was quite impossible to say an approving word about the clergy. And yet to us, who have survived the Archipelago, those monks certainly seem angels. Though having every opportunity of eating their bellies full, they, in the Golgotha–Crucifixion Monastery, permitted themselves fish, itself a fast dish, only on the great holidays. Despite the opportunity to sleep whenever they pleased, they kept vigil for nights on end, and (in that same small monastery) day long, year long, and in

perpetuity, read the Psalter around the clock and prayed for all
Orthodox Christians, living and dead.

(op. cit. Part III, Ch. II, note 1)

The monastic life, with its disciplines of prayer, fasting and
keeping vigil, is not remote from the lives of those unjustly
imprisoned. The white martyrdom of witness, of endurance in
the spiritual conflict, is not of a totally different order from the
white martyrdom of those who have 'survived the Archipelago',
and the red martyrdom of those hundreds of thousands who have
not.

In a most profound study of Solzhenitsyn's writings, *The Spirit
of Solzhenitsyn* (Search Press 1976, henceforth referred to as *SS*
in the references), Olivier Clément combines the insights of
Orthodox spirituality and theology with those of literary criticism.
He selects various themes such as 'Death and the Meaning of Life',
'Being as Sacrament' and 'Conscience in the Image of God' and
shows how these themes, well known to Christian spirituality, are
re-expressed in a wholly original and often remarkably beautiful
way by Solzhenitsyn. Clément focuses, with a close-up lens, into
a series of still pictures for contemplation, details from the vast
moving panorama of Solzhenitsyn's novels and other writings. He
traces the literary use of recurrent images, giving one a unified
vision of Solzhenitsyn's message: that death is always present in
the midst of life; that existence is nevertheless to be wondered at;
and that every human face is a way to joy, truth and the Divine.

In Clément's book also, I found confirmation of the relevance of the monastic life to this particular moment in history.
I quote:

The historical experience of evil is still alive [in Eastern Europe].
But that experience, destructive as it is for so many, has a
terrible fecundity of its own in the case of the few. It is as
though history were leading millions of men along a narrow
route from which there is no escape: that of the most severe
discipline. When men no longer offer sacrifice total wars break
out. Wherever monasteries disappear, there prison doors open

to innocent people, and some of them become monks. If a civilization based on the pursuit of happiness knows no discipline but the dedication of sportsmen, weekend yogis and the devotees of the latest slimming craze, a tragic sequence of events imposes on the 'living dead' a new deprivation, fasting, continence, and what is known in Orthodox spirituality, as the *memento mori*. And yet, in the light of this spirituality . . . the *memento more* can become a kind of resurrection.

(*SS*, Part I. 1. 'The camp, war, cancer', pp. 10, 11)

Monks in the Orthodox tradition have been called the 'risen ones' and it behoves us Western monastics not to succumb to the temptations of a superficial 'with-it-ness' and thus to bypass the being 'nailed to the cross of our Order' – as a medieval work, *A Talkyng of the Love of God*, puts it. What Solzhenitsyn says of the 'living dead' who have 'survived the Archipelago' must also be able to be said of those living the monastic life: that they have experienced a *metanoia*, not just in the sense of repentance, but as man's *return* to his own deepest centre where he can find again the image of God. When Solzhenitsyn adds, 'it is as if they bore some luminous sign on their foreheads, or stigmata on their feet and palms' (*Cancer Ward*, ch. 34), one is reminded of the allegory of the life of the monk as it is given in the Athonite *Painter's Guide* of 1458:

Draw a cross and set on it a monk . . . His feet are to be nailed to the footboard of the cross, his eyes and mouth are to be closed . . . And in his hands he holds lighted candles . . . And above the inscription which is at the head of the monk [write] this: Let it not be mine to boast but in the cross of my Lord . . . And also draw Jesus in the midst of clouds at the head of the cross, and on his breast an open Gospel with the words: He who wishes to come after me, let him take up his cross and follow me.[1]

Like the Christian monks, those who 'become monks' when the 'prison doors open', learn the necessity of a radical detachment in order to attain to true freedom. 'It is in the nature of man that as long as he is alive there is always something that can be taken away from him' (*The First Circle*, ch. 84), and for the majority of prisoners it is this fear of deprivation that his captors work upon and which can be used to destroy him as a human being. But the system can go too far and become self-defeating. 'You only have power over people so long as you don't take *everything* away from them. But when you've robbed a man of *everything* he's no longer in your power – he's free again' (ibid. ch. 17). For the few there may be a conscious choice which can turn the circumstances of evil into a form of asceticism, a stripping down of life to bare bones and a striving for what is essential. So those who had chosen to descend lower than the first circle of hell, to confront death in the camps, 'were at peace within themselves. They were as fearless as men who have lost everything they ever had – a fearlessness hard to attain but enduring once it is reached' (ibid. ch. 87).

Monks also are those who seek for the 'one thing necessary ... doing violence in everything to the death which impregnates our lives, and of which they become acutely conscious: a violence of *obedience*, which gives freedom from the ego and its characterisations; a violence of *poverty*, which gives freedom from all possessions, in every sense of this word; a violence of *chastity* which makes way for the first two freedoms and ensures the crucifixion and transformation of *eros* by *agape* ... For the monk the most precious thing in the world is the comprehended love of God. The monk is he who welcomes this love which seems non-existent and empty for most men.'[2]

In Part II of *The Spirit of Solzhenitsyn*, 'Towards Spiritual Awareness', Clément devotes three chapters to 'Eros and love'. I would like to draw from those chapters and make a further connection from Solzhenitsyn's insights into *eros* and love with the monastic understanding of chastity. In Clément's view, it is monasticism which 'could give the true, fully "paracletic" meaning and direction' to that basic drive of *eros* which man shares with the rest of God's animate creation.[3]

Solzhenitsyn is fully aware of the ambiguity of *eros*. 'It can transcend itself and achieve fulfilment in the communion of persons; between a man and woman it can become the language of immensity and silence, the power of mutual service. But by becoming objectified it can also drive them back into their respective solitudes, supplant the absolute, and then sink back, having reduced an hour, a month or a lifetime even, to ashes' (*SS*, p. 72).

The encounter of Oleg and Zoya in *Cancer Ward* expresses this ambivalence. The 23 year-old Zoya, nurse and medical student, is full of good health and vital energy. Like most of her friends she 'believed that everything possible should be grabbed from life immediately and with both hands' (op. cit. ch. 6). She tries to enjoy life to the full but she remains dissatisfied. Her grandmother has told her that she does not need a handsome suitor but a *good* one, a man of integrity. Will this be Oleg, a patient recovering from cancer, a man who has been through the camps and is now exiled 'in perpetuity'? Oleg talks about his life, tacitly asking if Zoya will understand and would be prepared to join him in exile. But she cannot grasp the depths of his experience and so misunderstanding and passion grow up between them. Their first kiss lacks the innocence of true love; each is evaluating the experience and Oleg feels that Zoya's eyes are predatory and he is the prey. Clément comments: 'This is why eroticism makes for such terrifying loneliness . . . "Their mouths joined again. They wanted to drain each other dry" − to get something and give nothing of themselves. Soon, however, mechanical pleasure becomes habit, need, passion; and passion, because it fails to integrate a person's inner drives into a process of genuine exchange and mutual service, leads, paradoxically to emptiness. Two isolated people, reaching out pathetically to a form of satisfaction through which each merely consumes the other without bringing healing: two people who, precisely because of their isolation, are strangers to the suffering of others. Passion might well be defined as the opposite of compassion' (*SS*, pp. 75, 76).

This is illustrated by the episode of the oxygen cylinder. Oleg is like one possessed, 'thinking about this girl, this woman, this "bit of skirt" . . .' (Note how she is diminished from a person to an object.) Although Zoya is on duty they use the need to refill an oxygen balloon as an excuse to get away together. Oleg and Zoya are completely immersed in each other; 'although the balloon in her hands was needed for the sick man, to prevent him suffocating, they'd already forgotten about him.' At last, 'the gay, multi-coloured wheel of their game' rolls to its rest and they remember to switch off the oxygen just before the balloon bursts. 'The last few cubic centimetres of air in the doomed man's balloon had been no more than a pretext for going off into a corner together and getting to know each other's kisses.' Their unmindfulness of another's suffering calls forth a terrible word from Solzhenitsyn who says of the dying man: 'He was still alive but there were no living men around him' (*Cancer Ward*, ch. 18).

As in the marital relationship *eros* can become 'the language of immensity and silence', so for the monk it can become the 'dynamism, the language, the silence of personal love'. By the monk's struggle for purity of heart his *eros*, instead of being allowed to 'supplant the absolute' is opened up to the Holy Spirit and is transfigured by being filled with *his* divine energy. Whereas passion 'fails to integrate a person's inner drives into a process of genuine exchange and mutual service', the life of vowed chastity is an offering of the whole being to God; all one's creative faculties are, by it, submitted to God for their re-creation in Christ. It is a process of integration, a coming together into wholeness as a person, of which the fruit is a genuine availability to others and a genuine compassion. Like his Lord, the monk will not be a stranger to suffering, and all the world's sorrow will have a place in his heart. The saying of St Irenaeus, 'the glory of God is a living man', should be supremely true of the monk.

Solzhenitsyn has both 'survived the Archipelago' and made a remarkable recovery from cancer, and these experiences have marked him deeply. Clément suggests that they have affected Solzhenitsyn's approach to the mystery of *eros*. Because his heart has been purified by the nearness of death the old distinction between pure and impure has been swept away and there remains in its place a sense of the innocence of the flesh with a corresponding awareness of the terrible freedom of the individual. Clément perceives how 'each of us is inwardly aware of a pull, an impersonal *eros* . . . Each is inwardly aware also of the

Christian revelation of the person and of an unsatisfied longing for communion. If Solzhenitsyn roundly condemns all mechanical eroticism and the violence which prostitution does to women . . . he speaks gratefully of the gift a woman can make of her body, in a brief encounter, to a man who has been crushed by life in the camps or by sickness' (*SS*, p. 69). On the day Oleg Kostoglotov is discharged from the Cancer Ward he is pushed by the crowd on a tram very close to the body of a young girl who makes no attempt to move despite his grotesque appearance. Solzhenitsyn describes Oleg as remembering gratefully the curls on the back of the girl's neck; her face he had not even been able to see. Amid all his impressions of the beauty and freshness of creation this momentary contact with the girl's body is like a gift of new life to Oleg.

Those who are committed to a life of chastity have to experience the 'unsatisfied longing for communion' exclusively with another person, but while it is a costing knowledge it is not a negative one for it opens the heart outwardly to all men and inwardly to God. In the section on Celibacy and Prayer in his book *Teach us to Pray*, André Louf succeeds in articulating what is experienced inwardly:

When somebody freely embraces celibacy for Jesus' sake, and on behalf of prayer, then, in his body and in his sexual dynamic, something occurs that both restructures his whole person and intensifies prayer and his bond with Jesus. If this were not to happen, celibacy would be a terrible hazard and in many cases could only make for a stunted affective life . . . Our celibacy must be a sign that the new creation is beginning to dawn and that God has drawn close to man. Sexual abstinence for Jesus' sake presupposes a specific capacity for love – a widening, enlarging process so far out of the ordinary run of things that one is bound to call it charismatic. This happens in two directions. First *outwards*, towards greater universality. Virginity creates the possibility of entering into a love-relationship with all human beings. The unmarried person's family is the whole of mankind, the good as well as the bad, who are cherished and preserved by the Father. Sexual abstinence also enlarges the scope of our love

inwardly towards the deep interiority of our heart . . . Celibacy
can open up a path to prayer . . . prayer is assisted by the sexual
solitariness of man and woman . . . Through celibacy and prayer
man and woman find their other half in God.[4]

Vera Gangart, one of the doctors in *Cancer Ward*, may be
seen as typifying Solzhenitsyn's insight into a woman's capacity
to resist, because of her basic concern with people rather than
ideas, the moral degradation of her position in Soviet life and
the conditioning Marxist thought without losing her femininity.
This is how Clément, quoting Solzhenitsyn, describes Vera:

> The patients 'had become *her* patients . . . her own permanent
> living charges who trusted her and waited on the encourage-
> ment of her voice and the comfort of her glance.' In fact
> her grave, gentle, profoundly feminine beauty helped her to
> encourage her patients 'with glances and smiles to make up
> for their finding themselves inside this notorious cancer circle'.
> Her watchful brown eyes were indeed, for the patients, 'the eyes
> of a doctor', but they were also 'the eyes of a very old friend'
> – a friend indicating a personal relationship that transcends the
> difference between the sexes. Her 'severity is touched with
> softness . . .' it is 'somehow melodic and based on harmony'.
> Her femininity is preserved intact yet 'methodically' integrated
> into a personal vocation and service. (*SS*, p. 66)

This description reminded me of one of our Night Office
readings from *Die Ewige Frau* by Gertrud von le Fort: 'Because
it is only a child, poor and abandoned, the world needs to find
the mother in woman . . . [who] in silence bears and gives and
ever begins over again, triumphing over the limits of the material
by virtue of humble submission to earthly matter . . . conquering
day by day simply by making life bearable.' This is the vocation
not only of the married woman, the physical mother, but also of
those committed to celibacy, as Vera Gangart was out of fidelity
to her dead fiancé, or as the nun is by her vow of chastity.
Our chastity should similarly enable our essential womanhood

to flower and our innate capacity for motherhood to operate in healing and constructive ways.

> The true monk is he whom the beauty of Christ always draws in the light of the Spirit. He crucifies his *eros* and sees it rise again in a personal love. *Eros* then becomes entirely creative, a power not only of natural birth but also of regeneration. Monastic ascesis makes it possible to go beyond the element of capture and possession which is inherent in sexual life, so as to transform *eros* into openness, a tenderness of the whole being, spiritual paternity.[5]

Solzhenitsyn says that Vera Gangart's lips 'were made, as all lips are, for kissing, yet they had other more important work to do: to sing of brightness and beauty' (*Cancer Ward*, ch. 34). Tradition calls the monk 'equal to an angel', not in the sense of an asexual angelism, but because the monk exists to proclaim with his whole being the Psalmist's words, 'I will sing to the Lord as long as I live; I will sing praise to my God while I have my being'. The monk, like the angel, is to be a singer of God's glory of *his* 'brightness and beauty'. (Solzhenitsyn is probably not unaware of this tradition when he refers to the monks of Solovki as 'angels'.)

Solzhenitsyn has much to say about *eros* and love when it is denied its physical expression. One of the most moving characters in *Cancer Ward* is Elizaveta Anatolyevna. She is one of those unobtrusive people whose self-effacing concern for others makes it easy for them to overlook her. 'The more uncomplainingly she worked, the less notice they took of her . . . As the two-thousand-year-old saying goes, you can have eyes and still not see' (*Cancer Ward*, ch. 34). She had been deported with her husband and daughter, who died in exile. Then after their release her husband was re-arrested and she is left alone with a small son. Although she is highly intelligent and formidably well-read, this 'history' has forced her to become a hospital orderly. Her love for her husband remains constant and Solzhenitsyn describes her as 'hanging on a single thread, a single thread of hope' for the hypothetical letter she longs to receive from him. Clément comments that 'hers is not that tense kind of expectation which would drive her deeper into her distress, but an expectation full of faith which strengthens her inner resources and alerts her to the suffering of others. With quiet devotion to duty she "crawls under the beds to wash the floor", carried "anything heavy, inconvenient or dirty"' (*SS*, p. 92).

This presents the fairly standard picture of the religious Sister sublimating her natural desires into service of the poor and suffering. In our own contemplative life, while the vow of chastity will express itself in loving service of one's neighbour through the ministry of prayer, there is also something else. Contrary to much modern thought, which understands sexuality as necessarily implying physical relations between men and women for completeness, the vocation to a life of vowed chastity witnesses to the fact that sexuality can play a rightful part in all human relationships, other than a physical one, and that it can be integrated into all the areas of one's life. As with Elizaveta Anatolyevna, love, when it is denied its physical expression, does not just wither and die, but it broadens out to reach the crying need of all humanity. It expresses itself in a genuine 'bearing of one another's burdens' – as the weekday Chapter at Sext constantly reminds us.

Gleb and Nadya Nerzhin only shared one year of married life together before they were separated first by the war and then by Gleb's unjust imprisonment. After a rare half-hour meeting in the Leforto Prison, which Clément describes as 'by its very reticence one of the most intense love scenes in all literature' (*SS*, p. 88), their love for one another is deeply reborn. But the testing time comes *afterwards*, and I am immensely grateful to Clément for setting side by side in two of his 'portraits' this meeting of Gleb and Nadya with their experiences on the day following, which are separated by three hundred pages in *The First Circle*.

Before he knew of his wife's visit Gleb had arranged an assignation with one of the free workers, but 'after his yesterday's meeting with Nadya, his hands and lips were clean, and it seemed impossible to him now to go up to Simochka, draw her close to him and kiss her.' She is obviously upset by his 'distance', and this pierces Gleb's own defences. His refound love for Nadya helps him to appreciate Simochka more truly, without despising her, and he ends by asking her forgiveness. Solzhenitsyn describes

Gleb as he 'pressed his forehead to the window again, and looked out into the darkness. And, as sometimes happens when one looks at scattered lights at night, thinking of something else, they ceased to be those of the Moscow suburbs; he forgot where and what they were, they assumed a new significance . . .' They spoke of the light of his new found faith in God and love for his wife (*The First Circle*, ch. 47).

Nadya meanwhile, back in the hostel where she has to conceal the fact of her marriage and of her visit to the prison, is profoundly depressed by Gleb's hint that he would not be freed for a long time, perhaps never. A male friend of her own age calls in to see her and for a moment she allows herself to enjoy the comfort of his physical closeness, until a whisper is torn out of her to the effect that her husband is alive and in prison and that she has seen him. Shchagov, her friend, rushes out and Nadya goes over to the window, reaching out to feel the cool panes against her palms. Solzhenitsyn says she stands there, 'like someone crucified on the black cross of the window . . .' 'She could see a long row of street lights stretching away in the darkness, as though into the future – a future for which she had no will to live.' Suddenly Shchagov bursts in with a bottle and two glasses: 'Well, soldier's wife! Don't lose heart! . . . Let's drink to the resurrection of the dead' (ibid, ch. 47).

Clément comments: 'This is the mystery of conjugal fidelity in physical separation. Nadya, who "does not believe in God", has just participated in the death-resurrection of the unknown God who awaits us in the darkness even of hell. Two windows open on the same night. Between the separated couple there is only a night – a sign of crucifixion and resurrection' (*SS*, p. 92).

The mystery of conjugal fidelity is balanced by the mystery of monastic stability – both strengthen and support each other in the Body of Christ. It probably takes a lifetime to plumb the depths and heights of the image of *night* in relation to chastity as fidelity in relationship. Our monastic life is lived against this recurring rhythm of night; it is, as it were, a refrain to our life as it is to St John of the Cross's beautiful 'Song of the soul that delights in knowing God by faith', '. . . Although 'tis night'. This night is for us too a sign of both crucifixion and resurrection. As another of our Night Office lessons puts it: 'Celibacy is a fight, an *agon*, like Christ's passion. It may entail all the pangs and anguish Christ experienced on the cross. But the Christian virgins are comforted by the knowledge that the pains of their state of life are nothing but the pains of the death of their Master, the birth pangs of the new world, of the progressive stripping of the flesh from the old man, as the new Adam rises slowly to the new life in the Spirit.'[6] And as the first Alleluia sung in the Easter Vigil 'rises above the grave of Adam' with 'the blood of Christ on its wings', 'so is the whole life of Christians: a gentle, quiet song of joy which meets the rise of day in the midst of the suffering night of time.'[7]

But night, as we have seen, is not only the time of separation and suffering; it is also the time of union:

> O night you were the guide!
> O night more desirable than dawn!
> O dark of night you joined
> Belovéd with belov'd one,
> Belov'd one in Belovéd now transformed.[8]

Finally, from Clément's book, I would like to quote his commentary on Solzhenitsyn's play, *The Love Girl and the Innocent*.

Lyuba's parents were peasants who had the use of a family allotment. The entire family was deported when the land was collectivised and both father and mother died in the upheaval. In order to survive Lyuba took to prostitution, and in the camp where she has ended up she has become more of a 'love-girl' than ever. As far as she is concerned, men are 'only after one thing', so that she herself has been reduced to that one thing. Then a young officer, Nemov, who has been arrested for some unspecified reason, discovers her and offers her tenderness and personal love. He does not ask for her body, but simply that she should be there because with her he feels good, free . . . And so for one week they live this true liberating love at every level of their being, including the physical, and during that time he is rescued from the 'mist' in which he had been stumbling since his arrest, while she is set free from the objectivization of her own body . . . Then she makes a terrible sacrifice: she agrees to go and live with the camp doctor, a sensual petty tyrant, knowing that in so doing she will be able to save Nemov. She gets his name struck off the list of those to be transferred to a camp from which no one ever returns and cares for him after an accident. For him she is a lost woman in every sense of the term . . . she surrenders her life in order to save him. Her last words, spoken on the threshold of her place of humiliation are: 'He's alive.'

(*SS*, p. 80)

That quality of total disregard for self, a willingness to 'lay down one's life' for others is the quality asked of the Christian celibate. Lyuba's last words recall Guerric of Igny's first Easter Sermon. He uses an Old Testament text: 'Jacob's spirit revived, and he said, It is enough for me if Joseph my son be yet living.' Guerric says: 'in this you will know that your spirit has fully come to life in Christ, if it can say sincerely, "It is enough for me that Jesus lives".' Thomas Merton, commenting on the sermon, says: 'There you have the doctrine of pure love packed into a very short phrase', and he re-translates Guerric's next sentence: 'If Jesus himself is absent from me, provided he is living, anyway for himself, I don't care about me.'[9] That is to be the whole trend of our lives vowed to chastity: '*He's alive – I don't care about me.*'

In conclusion, I can only hope, like St Augustine, that 'one who loves will understand' the connections I have tried to make. It is perhaps significant that *Lyuba* is the Russian word for love in the sense of *agape* so, in the sacrifice of this 'love-girl', we are shown that *eros* and *agape* are not to be set in opposition to one another. Olivier Clément, writing as a theologian, sees *eros*, in its root, as the impulse of the Holy Spirit within us, 'a tension towards the highest life, a tension which makes of true man a "man of desire" (Rev. 22:17)'. Therefore, he writes:

At the same time as we of the laity are called to live a renewed experience of the marital relationship, it behoves monks not to flee from *eros*, but to penetrate its meaning, to transfigure it integrally into an impatience for the Parousia – an impatience which was so very evident in early monasticism. The greatest and most rigorous ascetics, like St John Climacus, and the most profound mystics, like Dionysius, have deciphered the meaning of *eros* which, they say, must not be destroyed but changed. *Eros*, for them, constitutes the 'pneumatic' spirit of created nature tending towards its origin and its end. Having become disordered in the world of alienations it is called to become in the Spirit the dynamism, the language, the silence of personal love ... Opposed to natural desire (*eros*) made absolute and impersonal, the practice of chastity opens the way for the fulfilment of *eros*, in what Climacus means by the expression 'love (*eros*) for God'. 'O that physical love', he says, 'might be seen as a model for the love of God.' And again, 'Blessed is he who has no less violent a passion for God than that of the lover restless for his beloved.' ... Only this grounding of *eros* in the invisible can communicate, particularly to those who are committed to the ascesis of marriage, a true understanding of chastity as spiritual integrity, as an integration of *eros* in a personal relationship of fidelity.[10]

> *Many waters cannot quench love,*
> *neither can the floods drown it;*
> *if a man would give all the substance of his house for love,*
> *it would be utterly contemned.*

NOTES

1. Philip Sherrard, *Athos, the Mountain of Silence*, OUP 1960, p.71.
2. Olivier Clément 'The Holy Spirit and Monasticism Today', trans. CSWG, 1978.
3. Ibid.
4. André Louf, *Teach us to Pray*, DLT 1974, p.64.
5. Clément, op. cit.

6. Lucien Legrand, *The Biblical Doctrine of Virginity*, Geoffrey Chapman 1963, pp.69f.

7. Aemiliana Löhr, *The Mass through the Year*, Vol.II, p.64. Longmans 1959, p.64.

8. R. Nicholson (trans.) 'The Dark Night', from G. Brenan, *St John of the Cross, His Life and Poetry*, CUP 1973, pp.145-6.

9. *Cistercian Studies*, 1972:1.

10. Clément, op. cit.

Sister Edna Monica entered SLG in 1960. She is at present Prioress at the Convent of the Incarnation, Fairacres, Oxford.

Time: Prison or Path to Freedom?

*University Sermon, Preached in St Mary the Virgin, Oxford,
on Sunday 11 June 1989*

BISHOP KALLISTOS OF DIOKLEIA

See then that you walk circumspectly, not as fools but as wise,
redeeming the time. (Eph. 5:15-16)

Circle, Line, Spiral

It is a striking fact, easily overlooked, that in the New Testament
Jesus Christ begins his public ministry by speaking of time, and
that he likewise refers to time in the last conversation that he
has with his disciples at the very end of his earthly life. 'The
time is fulfilled' (Mark 1:15): so Christ commences his preaching,
while immediately before his Ascension he says to the eleven: 'It
is not for you to know the times or seasons which the Father has
fixed by his own authority' (Acts 1:7). Both at the outset and at
the conclusion of the story, the question of time confronts us:
time as fulfilled in Christ, time as a mystery still hidden in God.
What, then, do we mean by time?

Since the theme of time is in this way deeply embedded in
the Gospel narrative, we cannot dismiss the question as no more
than a speculative issue, of interest merely to the professional
philosopher. It is a matter that concerns each one of us personally.
Philip Larkin's query is posed to us all:

> *What are days for?*
> *Days are where we live.*
> *They come, they wake us*

> *Time and time over . . .*
> *Where can we live but days?*[1]

'What are days for?' The question is not simply 'What is time? but 'What is time *for*?' We are concerned not just with the abstract essence of time but with its practical effect on our lives. What are we to do about time, what are we to make of it?

Oscar Cullmann, in his classic work *Christ and Time*, offers two basic images of time. It may be seen as cyclical, as a circle, ring or wheel; or else it may be seen as linear, as a straight path, a river or an arrow. Without asserting too sharp a dichotomy between Hellenism and Judaism, it may be said that the first manner of envisaging time is characteristically Greek – in Aristotle's words, 'For indeed time itself seems to be a sort of circle'[2] – while the second approach predominates in Hebraic and Iranian thought. Not that the two symbols need be mutually exclusive, for they both embody an aspect of the truth. The image of the circle reflects the recurrent rhythms in the world of nature, the line expresses our sense of time as direction, progress and evolution. What strikes us at once is that these symbols are both alike double-edged. The circle of time may be felt as redemptive, as the means of our return to the golden age, to the lost paradise; or it may be viewed as meaningless repetition, as boredom and futility. It may serve as an image of celestial eternity – Henry Vaughan's 'great ring of pure and endless light' – or it may be a sign of hell, a closed and vicious circle. So it is also with linear time. It is true that the line may be strictly horizontal, and therefore neutral. But equally it may be seen as oblique or sloping, and in that case inclined either upward or downward. Interpreted positively, the line of time becomes a path of ascent to the summit of the holy mountain; understood negatively, it signifies deterioration and decline, 'downhill all the way': *Facilis descensus Averni* . . . Once more the image is equivocal.

A better symbol of time than either the circle or the line is surely the spiral, combining elements from both the other figures, yet avoiding their more blatant defects. The spiral, more truly than the circle or the line, reflects the basic patterns in the physical universe, from the movement of the galaxies to the folds in the human cerebral cortex. It includes the cyclic rhythms of nature, yet in the case of the spiral the circle is not closed but suggests continuous advance towards a goal. Above all, the spiral has the advantage of being – at any rate in some instances – three-dimensional, thus expressing our post–Einsteinian sense of living in a space-time continuum. St Dionysius the Areopagite regarded the spiral as the highest type of movement, the form most befitting the angelic powers,[3] and that strange prophetic figure of twelfth-century Italy, Joachim of Fiore, thought the same; and I am inclined to agree with them. Once more, however, the question confronts us: what kind of spiral? For spirals can be either descending or ascending, or rather they may be both these things at once, as the sailor discovered in Poe's story, *A Descent into the Maelstrom*. What, then, is to be our perception of time's spiral: a descending vortex, sucking us down into annihilation, or the never-ending dance of love, drawing us 'farther up and farther in'?

Enemy or Friend?

Our experience of time, as these three symbols indicate, is deeply ambivalent. How are we to regard time: as enemy or friend, as our prison or our path to freedom? Which aspect do we find predominant in its double-edged impact upon us: anguish or healing, terror or hope, decay or growth, separation or relationship? If the second edition of *The Oxford Dictionary of Quotations* can be trusted as a guide, time has commonly been seen more as a threat than as an enrichment. We find Shakespeare castigating 'envious and calumniating time . . . that bald sexton, Time'; in Ben Jonson's eyes time is 'that old bald cheater'; 'Time with a gift of tears,' writes Swinburne, while Tennyson calls time 'a maniac scattering dust'. Others, it is true, refer to time in more constructive terms as a 'gardener' or a 'physician', but they are minority voices. For Isaac Watts, time with its irreversible flow brings about a sense of loss and unreality:

> *Time, like an ever-rolling stream,*
> 　*Bears all its sons away:*
> *They fly forgotten, as a dream*
> 　*Dies at the opening day.*

An equally sombre view is to be found in the main biblical work devoted to the theme of time, Ecclesiastes. In the opening chapter the Preacher sees time as vain repetition, as the cause of 'weariness' and disillusion (Eccles. 1:2-9):

> *All is vanity . . .*
> *One generation passes away,*
> 　*and another generation comes . . .*
> *The wind blows to the south,*
> 　*and goes round to the north;*
> *round and round goes the wind,*
> 　*and on its circuits the wind returns.*
> *All streams run to the sea,*
> 　*but the sea is not full;*
> *to the place where the streams flow,*
> 　*there they flow again.*
> *All things are full of weariness . . .*
> 　*and there is nothing new under the sun.*

Taken as a whole, however, the scriptural attitude towards time is markedly less hostile than this. The Preacher himself in a later section links time with beauty and with eternity: 'For everything there is a time, and an appointed moment for every matter under heaven . . . He has made everything beautiful in its time; also he has put eternity into man's mind' (Eccles. 3:1, 11). In the New Testament this positive approach is reaffirmed. 'The time is fulfilled' (Mark 1:15): time is not pointless but purposive; Christ comes in the fullness of time. So far from being meaningless and arbitrary, time is something which 'the Father has fixed by his own authority' (Acts 1:7). St Paul speaks of 'the accepted time' or 'time of God's favour' (2 Cor. 6:2); time can be 'redeemed' (Eph. 5:16). God has made the 'ages' or 'aeons' of time (Heb. 1:12), and he is 'the king of the ages' (1 Tim. 1:17). There is no doubt about the biblical view: time is part of God's creation, and as such it is 'altogether good and beautiful' (Gen. 1:31, LXX).

Bisecting the World of Time

If we are to appreciate the beauty of time at its full value, then there are two basic truths that need to be kept in view. First, time and eternity are not opposed but interdependent, not mutually exclusive but complementary. Second, the meaning of time is to be found in relationship, in personal communion, in response and openness to others. Time is not to be interpreted merely in privative terms as a reflection of human finitude and a restriction on our liberty, but it is a positive expression of what it signifies to be a person, an indispensable precondition of human freedom and love. As regards both of these truths, the key to the right understanding of time is provided by Christ's Incarnation.

Time and eternity are not opposed. When Spinoza maintains, 'Eternity cannot be defined by time or have any relation to it',[4] the second part of this statement, at any rate, is definitely open to question. Indeed, the Incarnation involves precisely an 'intersection of the timeless with time', to use T.S. Eliot's phrase in *The Four Quartets*.[5] As he puts it in *The Rock*, Christ's birth is an event within time and yet transforming time:

> Then came, at a predetermined moment, a moment in time and of time,
> A moment not out of time, but in time, in what we call history: transecting, bisecting the world of time, a moment in time but not like a moment of time,
> A moment in time but time was made through that moment: for without the meaning there is no time, and that moment of time gave the meaning.[6]

'Transecting, bisecting the world of time': Eliot's point is brought out vividly in the *Protevangelion* or *Book of James*, when Joseph speaks of time as standing still at the moment of the Nativity:

Now I Joseph was walking, and I walked not. And I looked up into the air and saw the air in amazement. And I looked up to the pole of heaven and saw it standing still, and the birds of the heaven without motion. And I looked upon the earth and saw a dish set, and workmen reclining beside it, and their hands were in the dish: and they that were chewing did not chew, and they that were lifting the food did not lift it, and they that were putting it into their mouth did not put it in, but the faces of them all were looking upward. And behold there were sheep being driven, and they did not move forward but stood still; and the shepherd lifted his hand to strike them with his staff, and his hand remained in the air. And I looked at the stream of the river and saw the mouths of the kids upon the water, and they did not drink. Then suddenly all things moved onward on their course.[7]

What can be affirmed to a supreme degree concerning the time of the Incarnation is likewise true, at least potentially, of every moment of time. At the Incarnation eternity transects time in a unique manner. Yet each moment of time is also open to eternity; at each moment it is possible for eternity to break into the temporal sequence, assuming time into itself and so transforming it. Eternity is not simply outside the moments of time but at the heart of each moment; and this eternity, present within time, gives to time its true value. 'Eternity is as much in time as it is above time', writes the contemporary Romanian Orthodox theologian, Archpriest Dumitru Staniloae, who has devoted particular attention to the Christian significance of time.[8]

Plato was not far from the truth when he spoke of time as a moving image of eternity.[9] Time and eternity – and, by the same token, space and infinity – do not contradict but complete one another. Time and space, while modalities of the created order, are rooted in God's eternal, uncreated life and find their fulfilment there. Between time and eternity there exists, to use the phrase of the French Orthodox author Olivier Clément, 'a marriage bond', *un rapport proprement nuptial*.[10] In the words of St Maximos the Confessor, 'The inner principles [*logoi*, 'reasons'] of time abide in God.'[11] 'The divine eternity', writes Fr Staniloae, '. . . carries within itself the possibility of time, while time carries within itself the possibility of participating in eternity.' Eternity is turned towards time and goes out to meet it; and time, when taken up into eternity, is not annihilated but transfigured.

Time as Freedom to Love

Let us turn now to our second point. Time from a Christian perspective is one of the means whereby God evokes and guarantees our created human freedom, our freedom to love. The notion of freedom − both divine freedom and human freedom − is fundamental to the Christian doctrine of creation. 'God is truly present and operative only in freedom,' claims Berdyaev. 'Freedom alone should be recognized as possessing a sacred quality.'[12] As Kierkegaard has rightly insisted, 'The most tremendous thing granted to humans is choice, freedom.'[13] God created the world in freedom, and he willed that the beings whom he formed in his image should likewise be free. As a Trinitarian God, a God of shared interpersonal love, he desired that we humans in our turn should be joined to him in a relationship of mutual love. Mutual love, however, presupposes freedom, for where there is no voluntary choice there can be no love. Love cannot be constrained, but can only be tendered willingly; God is able to do anything except *compel* us to love him. Love comes always as an offer to which the beloved is invited to respond in freedom.

By creating in this way a world of persons capable of freely responding to him in love, God accepted to restrict, in some measure, the exercise of his omnipotence. He 'withdrew' as it were from his creation, 'distancing' himself so that his creatures might have room to love. Creation involves a divine self-limitation, what the sixteenth-century Jewish Kabbalist, Isaac Luria, termed *zimsum*, 'contraction' or 'concentration'.[14] In thus bringing into existence free persons with the power of rejecting him, God inevitably took a risk. But had he not taken a risk, there would have been a universe without love. As Vladimir Lossky observes, 'This divine risk, inherent in the decision to create beings in the image and likeness of God, is the summit of almighty power, or rather a surpassing of that summit in voluntarily undertaken powerlessness . . . He who takes no risks does not love.'[15]

This risk-taking or *kenosis* on God's part, inaugurated at the creation, came to its full expression at the Incarnation. In choosing to become a creature, the divine Creator embraced a situation of complete vulnerability, an entire and unreserved solidarity with us humans in our pain and brokenness. He willed to effect our salvation, not through any exercise of transcendent power, but through the utter powerlessness of his incarnate state: 'My strength is made perfect in weakness' (2 Cor. 12:9). Such exactly is the supreme paradox of Christology: God is never so strong as when he is most weak, never so truly divine as when he empties himself. St Gregory of Nyssa saw this clearly: 'The fact that the omnipotent nature should have been capable of descending to the humiliated condition of humanity provides a clearer proof of power than great and supernatural miracles . . . His descent to our lowliness is the supreme expression of his power.'[16] Nestorius made the same point: 'All greatness grows great by self-abasement, and not by exalting itself.'[17] And the reason why God chose to save us not by force but with our voluntary consent is specifically that he loves us and therefore desires us to be free.

It is in this context of freedom and love that the meaning of time can best be appreciated. Time is part of the 'distancing' or 'contraction' on God's side which makes it possible for us humans freely to love. It is, as it were, the interspace which enables us to move towards God unconstrained and by our voluntary choice. 'Behold I stand at the door and knock', says Christ; 'if anyone hears my voice and opens the door, I will come in to him and eat with him and he with me' (Rev. 3:20). God knocks, but does not break down the door; he waits for us to open. This *waiting* on God's part is exactly the essence of time: in Fr Staniloae's words, 'For God, time means the duration of the expectant waiting between his knocking on the door and our act of opening it.' God issues his appeal to human freedom: 'Whom shall I send, and who will go for us?' After that he awaits the voluntary response from our side: 'Then I said, "Here am I! Send

me"' (Isa. 6:8). Time is the interval between God's appeal
and our answer. We humans need this interval of time so as
freely to love God and one another; without the interval we
cannot engage in the dialogue of love. On the level of uncreated
divine freedom, the mutual love of the Trinity is an expression
of the *totum simul*, of eternal simultaneity, and so it is without any
interval of time. But on the level of created human freedom love
has to be learnt; and learning takes time, as we in this university
are only too well aware. Blake has well described our human
condition in his *Songs of Innocence*:

> And we are put on earth a little space,
> That we may learn to bear the beams of love.[18]

Time is thus an all-important dimension of our created personhood, the setting that makes it possible for us to choose love. It is
time that allows us to respond to God by our own free consent,
that enables our love to mature, that permits us to grow in love.
Space is to be understood in similar terms, as an expression of
God's self-distancing so that we may be free to respond to him
in love. It affords us, says Fr Staniloae, the possibility of 'free
movement . . . the freedom to draw near or to move away'.
Without time and space we cannot experience the 'between'
that unites in love the 'I' and the 'Thou'. If in our daily life we
commonly apprehend time very differently – not as relationship
but as separation, not as freedom but as fetters upon our liberty
– then that is because we are part of a fallen world in which
time has become linked with mortality and death. Yet, although
fallen, time is not totally so; even in our present condition we still
glimpse its primal significance as a 'time of gifts' and a contin-
ual miracle. And, because it is God's creation and as such is
'altogether good and beautiful', time is not to be repudiated
or ignored, but redeemed. Our goal is not timelessness but
time transfigured. It is true that in the Apocalypse the angel
proclaims, 'There shall be time no longer' (Rev. 10:6) – some
would render it 'There shall be no more delay' – but the time
that is to be abolished is the fallen time of death (cf. Rev.

21:4). For the Apocalypse also states that within the heavenly Jersualem there will be 'the tree of life with its twelve kinds of fruit, yielding its fruit *each month*' (Rev. 22:2). This can only mean that, in the eternal Kingdom of the age to come, the rhythms of cyclic time are not abolished but transformed.[19]

If the significance of time is to be found in relationship and love, it follows that true time is not simply that which is assessed mechanically by the clock or the calendar. True time is living, personal, existential, measured not by mere succession but by intention. True time is *kairos* rather than *chronos*, characterized not by the predetermined swing of the pendulum but by unpredictable yet decisive moments of opportunity, moments of disclosure filled with meaning when clock time stands still, as Joseph found in the *Protevangelion*, and when eternity breaks in. Time is not just a fixed, unvarying pattern imposed upon us from outside, but it can be recreated from within and used as an expression of our inner selves. We are in time, but time is also in us. We speak of 'wasting time' and 'killing time', but let us also give full value to the habitual phrases 'make time', 'give time' and 'save time'.

Without the Meaning there is no Time

In my reflections on time, as perhaps you will have noticed, a transition has taken place. Seeking to answer the question 'What is time?' I have been led to speak not just about time itself but about personhood, freedom and love. If time is discussed in the abstract and treated as a 'thing' that exists by itself, it proves ever more baffling and more elusive. St Augustine voices a difficulty familiar to us all: 'What is time? If no one asks me, I know; if I try to explain to an inquirer, I do not know.'[20] We can only begin to understand the nature of time when we take into account a whole series of other matters as well, such as our experiences of growth and decay, of being in relation, of learning to respond. 'Without the meaning there is no time': and there is no such thing as absolute time, for all time is related to persons and their inner experience. Time becomes intelligible only when set in the total context of life (and death) – indeed, the two terms 'time' and 'life' are in many respects virtually interchangeable.

Alike in terms of clock time and of personal time, it is time for me to end. It is the Incarnation, we have found, that provides us with a clue to the meaning of time. As 'the moment in and out of time', to use Eliot's words,[21] it shows us the interdependence of time and eternity; only *sub specie aeternitatis* does time acquire its authentic resonance and depth. And the Incarnation, as an act of love addressed to our human freedom, also indicates how time is to be understood in terms of personal relationship, of reciprocity and dialogue. Time, whether we choose to picture it as circle, line or spiral, is not a sexton or jailer, but the safeguard of our human personhood, the protector of liberty and love.

There are two moments in the Divine Liturgy which sum up these two aspects of time. The first is when the celebrant, immediately prior to the opening blessing, uses the words of the angels at the Incarnation, 'Glory be to God in the highest, and on earth peace . . .' (Luke 2:14); and then the deacon says to him, 'It is time for the Lord to act' (Ps. 118 [119]:126). It is the vocation of time to be open to eternity; time is fulfilled when God's eternity, God's action, breaks into the temporal sequence, as happened supremely at Christ's birth in Bethlehem, as happens also at every Eucharist. The second moment comes just before the Creed, when the deacon says to the people, 'Let us love one another . . .' and the people reply affirming their faith in the Father, Son and Holy Spirit. Such exactly is the true rationale of time: mutual love after the image of the Trinity.

NOTES

1. Philip Larkin, *Collected Poems* (London/Boston 1988), p.67.
2. Aristotle, *Physics* iv, 14 (223b29).
3. Dionysius the Areopagite, *The Divine Names* iv, 8 (*PG* 3, 704D). On the symbolism of the spiral, see Jill Purce, *The Mystic Spiral: Journey of the Soul* (London 1974).

4. Spinoza, *Ethics*, Part V, proposition xxiii, note: trans. A. Boyle (Everyman's Library: London 1910), p. 214. Quoted in Maurice Nicoll, *Living Time and the Integration of Life* (Boulder/London 1984), p. 132.

5. T.S. Eliot, 'The Dry Salvages', *The Complete Poems and Plays*, Faber and Faber (London 1969), pp.189–90.

6. Ibid., p. 160.

7. *Protevangelion* xviii, 2: ed. C. Tischendorf, *Evangelia Apocrypha* (Leipzig 1876), pp. 34–35; trans. M.R. James, *The Apocryphal New Testament* (Oxford 1924), p. 46 (translation adapted).

8. Staniloae discusses time and space in the first volume of his *Teologia dogmatica ortodoxa* (3 vols., Bucarest 1978), pp. 172–213. My quotations are taken from the English translation (as yet unpublished) by Ioan Ionita and Robert Barringer.

9. Cf. Plato, *Timaeus* 37d.

10 Olivier Clément, *Transfigurer le temps. Notes sur le temps à la lumière de la tradition orthodoxe* (Neuchâtel/Paris 1959), p. 54.

11 Maximos the Confessor, *Ambigua* (*PG* 91, 1164B).

12 Nicolas Berdyaev, *Dream and Reality: An Essay in Autobiography* (London 1950), p. 46.

13 Søren Kierkegaard, *Journals*, trans. A. Dru (London/Princeton 1938), p. 372 (translation adapted).

14 See Jürgen Moltmann, *The Trinity and the Kingdom of God* (London 1981), pp. 108–111.

15 Vladimir Lossky, *In the Image and Likeness of God* (Crestwood 1974), p. 214.

16 Gregory of Nyssa, *Catechetical Oration* 24.

17 Nestorius, *The Bazaar of Heracleides*, trans. G.R. Driver & L. Hodgson (Oxford 1925), p. 69 (translation adapted).

18 *Poetry and Prose of William Blake*, ed. G. Keynes (London 1948), p. 54.

19 Cf. Clément, op. cit., p. 72.

20 Augustine of Hippo, *Confessions* xi, 14.

21 T.S. Eliot, 'The Dry Salvages', op. cit., p. 190.

Bishop Kallistos of Diokleia has charge of the Greek Orthodox parish in Oxford, and is Spalding Lecturer in the University.

'And Sitteth on the Right Hand of the Father'

DERWAS J. CHITTY

' Stephen being full of the Holy Ghost, looked up steadfastly into heaven and saw the glory of God, and Jesus standing on the right hand of God, and said, "Behold I see the heavens opened, and the Son of Man standing on the right hand of God." '

What did St Stephen see? If he had seen a visual representation of God the Father, whom no man hath seen nor can see, with Jesus at his right hand, why then did he immediately, in echoing the Lord's first and last words from the Cross, transfer their address – 'Lord Jesus, receive my spirit', 'Lord, lay not this sin to their charge'? What he sees is indeed the Lord Jesus, but with the sense that beyond his visible human figure is all the eternity of the invisible Godhead. He, the Lord Jesus, is on the right hand of God's power, God's action in this world of time and space, opening heaven to us. So the Lord himself spoke in answer to the high priest – 'Art thou the Christ?' 'I am, and ye shall see the Son of Man sitting at the right hand of power, and coming with the clouds of heaven' – so St Mark has it: in St Matthew it is slightly altered, 'Henceforth ye shall see the Son of Man sitting at the right hand of power, and coming upon the clouds of heaven.' St Luke definitely brings it to an immediate fulfilment, 'From now shall the Son of Man be seated at the right hand of the power of God.'

The 'right hand of God' means then somehow the power of God. In fact, apart from the St Stephen passage, the Gospels and Acts give us only one example of the simple phrase, 'the right hand of God', and that in the appendix to St Mark (16:19). We probably should not stress the difference of use between the Gospels and

Acts, *ek dexion*, 'to the right', and the Epistles, *en dexia*, 'on the right hand'. In the Epistles we have 'on the right hand of God', simply, five times (Rom. 8:34; Eph. 1:20; Col. 3:1; Heb. 10:12; 1 Pet. 3:22); 'of the majesty' once (Heb. 8:1); 'of the throne of God' once (Heb. 12:2). Behind all these passages we have to remember the verse of the psalm quoted by our Lord, and recorded in each of the synoptic Gospels – and again quoted by St Peter at Pentecost, and in the Epistle to the Hebrews (1:13) – 'The Lord said unto my Lord, Sit thou on my right hand, until I make thine enemies thy footstool.'

So much for the New Testament basis of our credal assertion – 'ascended into heaven, and sitteth on the right hand of the Father'. I suppose normally we just think of it as the proclamation that the Church on earth has its head in heaven, 'whither Jesus Christ is gone before'. We think of the risen body as the disciples saw it after the resurrection – and are rather embarrassed at trying to place that on the throne of eternity. We are confused by thinking of the outward body rather than the whole man. But it is the whole man who is raised to the throne of eternity.

Even the Body is marked not only with the print of the nails and the spear-thrust. Its navel is there as the indelible mark of the cutting of the umbilical cord, separating the only-begotten Son and Word of God from the womb of her from whom for nine months he had drawn his whole bodily life. If even the outward body carries upon it an indelible record of its whole history, this is still truer of the complete person. So we retain in ourselves memories of whole life, which seem forgotten but can be revived. I had a friend slowly dying of a creeping paralysis which confined him to his chair; and I was constantly surprised at his detailed memory for places of which he had only a passing knowledge. We all know the stories of how in nearness to death a man finds his whole past life coming before him. But we can go further than this.

A projector casts an image upon a screen, but all the lights are on, and the image is invisible. Draw the curtain and turn out the lights, and the same image is bright. Our memory is like that image. Draw that curtain in death and there remains revealed the

picture of the life that has been, complete in every detail. The past
is no longer the past: it is present and real, though the fact that
life is growth and not just passage must surely give the final stage a
special importance as embracing all that has gone before. Even so
the humanity of Jesus which is taken up to the throne of heaven
is the whole of his human life. It is the babe of Bethlehem, the
boy in the Temple, the youth of the 'hidden years', who reigns
there, no less than the crucified young Prince of Glory. It was no
false instinct by which frequently in the history of the Church we
find the Christ in vision appearing as a child.

But here we meet the other truth. The throne of God is the
throne of eternity, to which all time is equally present, from the
beginning of creation to the final consummation. The right hand
of his power is God's working in all his creation. So when that
thirty-three-year life is taken up in its completeness to the right
hand of power, it is seen to spread its kingdom backwards as well
as forwards. In Salisbury Chapter-House, and again and again in
the early Middle Ages, the Creator is depicted as the Lord Jesus:
and whatever anthropomorphist dangers this may suggest, it is
more orthodox than Michaelangelo's greybeard Creator. The
Word speaking to Moses at the Burning Bush is the Lord, 'I
AM', who will be incarnate. And Moses on Sinai and Elijah on
Horeb are already over-leaping time, and speaking with Jesus on
the Mount of Transfiguration. He says, 'Before Abraham was, I
am.' He is the God of Abraham and of Isaac and of Jacob. He is
not a God of the dead but of the living.

Among the Fathers, St Ephraim the Syrian is, so far as I
know, the one who has best perceived this character of time,
reasoning that Adam, coming later than the rest of creation,
is yet older because all the rest was created with a view to
him; and that Christ who comes after John is yet before him
and before all things – 'He that cometh after me is preferred
before me, for he was before me.'

For a moment let us consider the possible implications of this
in regard to all creation. A single short life gives meaning to the
whole history of mankind. Mankind's short existence alone gives
sense and purpose to the far longer story of our planet. It is not a

long step from this to seeing our second-class planet as indeed at
the heart of God's purpose for this solar system; this comparatively
insignificant solar system for the whole galaxy; this galaxy for all
galaxies. Our imagination boggles: surely this planet cannot have
such a monopoly of uniqueness! But our reasoning is hard put to
it to say no. We can only say, It may be that God has other ways
in which he makes other parts of his creation central. What we
know is that in the only way that we can apprehend, our planet,
and mankind upon it, is indeed at the very heart of God's purpose.
The strange thing to us is the apparent universality of this law in
God's creation – that he is willing to create millions of apparent
failures for the sake of one success. From turbots' eggs to stars the
same rule seems to apply. And we shall never begin to understand
anything of God's ways unless we take him as we find him.

To return to the sitting at the right hand – it is the necessary counterpart to the Incarnation – 'Who for us men and
for our salvation came down from heaven, and was incarnate
by the Holy Ghost of the Virgin Mary, and was made man.'
Eternity was condensed into a short human life in order that
man might be given the freedom of eternity. God became man
in order that man might be deified.

He is Jesus, who lived as a man among men. But Jesus is the
Son of Man – the Captain of our salvation, the head of the body
of redeemed mankind. For true manhood must be corporate, not
individual. And apart from him, we have only to look at facts to
see how each life and all human lives put together fail to do more
than glimpse the eternity which lies beyond the prison-walls of
time. Taken into him, who alone embraces all time – 'Before
Abraham was, I am' – we are set free.

It is hereabouts, I think, that we find the necessity of the Virgin
birth and of the empty tomb – those two miracles compared with
which all others fade into insignificance, and which no trained
mind today would believe on the historical evidence alone, did
not something else in our hearts – certainly not just the outward
directives of the Church – command us not to deny them. For
the Virgin birth asserts that necessary integrated co-operation of
God and fallen man in bringing man's Saviour into the world,

while the empty tomb demonstrates that man's breaking out into eternity is already an accomplished fact.

The laws of Newtonian physics are absolutely valid within their own limits. Einstein came in to show that those limits were not commensurate with man's power to experiment. Even so, surely, we are to learn that other worlds which exist behind the world of our senses are not quite separate different levels of existence which never break in upon ours – but may be expected in fact to break in, sometimes imperceptibly, sometimes perceptibly, according to laws that we cannot know.

If it be true that each present moment contains the whole past, then we see the Cross as not just atoning for the past sins of the world in the sense of a forgiveness for what is past *and gone*, but as taking those sins, themselves still present, and transforming them into the means of his victory – even as the Cross itself, the greatest sin of the world, becomes the weapon of our salvation. That shocking phrase of the Exultet, '*O felix culpa*', is here triumphantly vindicated. And what is true of the history of mankind is true also in each life of ours. Our conversion is not just saying goodbye to sins that are past: it is the recognizing them as the nails which fix our Saviour to the Cross, and then seeing them taken by him to be the means of our salvation from them – and humbly allowing him so to heal us.

When all is gathered up in the consummation, the latent reality of each life that has been lived (and this includes, of course, its bodily reality) will be discovered in its completeness again – not just as a record of the past but as present reality (for to God all time is equally present) as time breaks out into eternity. The Judgement is simply the revealing of what we are – the ruthless revealing whether it is our will to be taken into the Kingdom which is the life of his Body, or whether we stand alone, outside, with no door opening to eternity.

'As in Adam all die, even so, in Christ shall all be made alive: but each in his own order: Christ the first-fruits; afterwards they that are Christ's at his coming. Then cometh the end, when he shall deliver up the Kingdom to God, even the Father, when he shall have brought to nought all rule and all authority and power. For he must reign, till he hath put all his enemies under his feet. The last enemy that is brought to nought is death . . . But when all things have been subjected unto him, then shall the Son also himself be subject unto him who subjected all things unto him, that God may be all in all' (1 Cor. 15:22-8).

'His Kingdom shall have no end.' This remains true especially as an assertion, with St Gregory of Nyssa, that there is no end of our growing – even of the angels! – growing into the fullness of the inexhaustible Godhead. But what St Paul is asserting is surely that within the peace of God, when all is returned to that, the subjection of the Son to the Father is no denial of his being of one Godhead with the Father, but is rather its proclamation.

Father Derwas Chitty (1901–71) devoted his life to the study of early Egyptian and Palestinian monasticism, summing up the fruits of forty years' research in his notable work, *The Desert a City*.

Spiritual Reading

A colloquy given to the Benedictines at St Benet's Hall, Oxford

SISTER EDMÉE SLG

A year or two ago, when I was studying the subject of Obedience and pondering the account of the Fall in connection with it, I lit upon a detail in the Hebrew text of Genesis 3 which, it seemed to me, opened the eyes of my understanding, not only in regard to the nature of the Fall but in regard to the resurrection appearances of Jesus. At the time I developed the detail in relation to obedience to the unseen world, and specifically in relation to obedience to the angelic world, but for this occasion I shall instead develop it in relation to the monastic practice of *Lectio Divina* or Spiritual Reading.

To set this detail in context we must start at the beginning of Genesis 3 with the entry of the serpent – a charming fellow who knows exactly how to chat up a girl. 'Did God say?' he asks Eve, in an easy conversational tone. And then, being, as the text says, 'more subtle than any beast of the field which the Lord God had made', he sets a trap for her by misquoting what God had actually said, and the woman falls into it – as any woman would – by putting him right. Having corrected him she is now vulnerable to him. A relationship is established and her seduction secured. The suggestion which the serpent makes penetrates her imagination – where all seduction takes place – and she is fully captured by his promise that in the day of her disobedience her eyes will be opened and she will see in a wonderfully new way.

Already she begins to see things from an altered perspective and with a beguiling clarity: 'So when the woman *saw* that the tree was good for food, and that it was a delight to the *eyes* . . .' Then the act of disobedience is committed and the first consequence, after Adam has meekly followed suit, is that 'the eyes of both were opened'. What eyes? 'The eyes that were then opened,' says Origen, 'were their senses, which they had been keeping shut, and rightly so, for fear they should be distracted and so prevented from seeing with their spiritual eyes.'[1] And because the eyes of their senses were now opened they at once saw what they had not seen before – that they were naked. And not only did they see themselves in this different way but they understood God differently for, as Adam confesses when God calls 'Where are you?', he has become afraid of him, and so he hides himself because, as he says, he is naked. And God, of course, knows the sin they have committed for now they see him with eyes which make them hide from him; and in their hiding from him, he becomes hidden to them.

God then enumerates to Adam and his wife the consequences to the human race of their disobedience, that, among other things, the pains of the woman in childbearing will be greatly multiplied, and that the man will eat bread in the sweat of his face. Then God clothes them – and here is the detail on which I shall hang the rest of this talk – in 'tunics [or garments] of skin', the word for skin being in the singular in the Hebrew text.

Now it was this singular form, even though it makes no odds whether it be singular or plural, which at once suggested to my understanding that an alteration of state takes place in Adam and Eve[2] and that after their eyes have been opened to the knowledge of good and evil God gives them the kind of bodies in which they will suffer the constraints their transgression has imposed on them – not that God slaughtered animals and processed their skins to provide them with clothes, as we are accustomed to imagine.[3] Adam and Eve have, in any case, already shown, on first seeing they were naked (3:7), that they are capable of clothing themselves. No, the skin with which God clothes them is intrinsic to their fallen nature which, in the light of this reading, further suggests that whereas before their sin Adam and Eve had enjoyed the benefits of incorporeality, and had been clothed, as St Ephrem the Syrian says, 'in garments of glory',[4] now they are confined in corporeality, in garments of skin.[5]

This view of the text immediately illuminates – for me, at least – the nature of Christ's incarnation, death and resurrection, for it would follow that Christ took upon himself precisely this 'garment of skin' that, by his life of obedience in the garment of disobedience, and by his nailing of it to the cross, the glorious body which God had created for the human race at the beginning might be restored to us – whence it becomes possible to understand what is meant by the 'resurrection of the body', which the appearances of Jesus after he had risen from the dead are at some pains to make clear to us.

But before considering those appearances, there is something to be gained from the Hebrew word for 'skin'. As a noun it consists of the same letters עוֹר as the verb 'to make blind', which the dictionary specifically links with the skin, giving 'whence blindness as cataract'. This verb in turn gives an adjective, usually used as a noun, 'the blind', and from this come the figurative meanings: the helpless, the groping, and also the dull, the unreceptive. And does not that wonderfully describe our state in relation to the invisible, spiritual world? For, whatever our original state, whether or not we fell from it into a different one, and whatever it was we were clothed in on so falling, the fact of the matter is that in relation to the invisible world we are – normally speaking – blind, notwithstanding that we affirm our belief in 'all that is, seen *and* unseen' every time we recite the Creed.

And so the sin of disobedience condemned us to a vision which, however clear at the level of the senses, is blind in relation to that of the spirit. Thereafter this blindness belongs to our fallen state and will only be healed in 'that day' when, Isaiah says, 'the eyes of the blind shall be opened' (29:18 and 35:5). And 'that day' has come. The obedience unto death of our Lord and Saviour Jesus Christ has effected the reversal of Adam's sin and given us the possibility of seeing with our spiritual eyes. But our seeing with our spiritual eyes remains only a possibility, a gift we cannot claim but which we must constantly be disposed to receive, in the same way that the prayer of contemplation comes to us only as a gift.

*   *   *

Now this possibility of seeing again with our spiritual eyes begins with Mary, just as the opening of our carnal eyes begins with Eve, and so it is to the disposition of Mary that we look first for a model for our own:

> And the angel came in unto her and said, Hail, thou that art highly
> favoured, the Lord is with thee; blessed art thou among women.
> And when she saw him she was troubled at his saying, and cast in
> her mind what manner of salutation this might be. (Luke 1:28-9)

The story of the Annunciation is recorded by Luke, the one who is called – and rightly – 'physician', for the dialogue between the angel and Mary is the precise counterpart, and the antidote therefore, to the dialogue between the serpent and Eve. For while Eve, as we have seen, receives the promise of the serpent in her imagination, Mary, troubled and fearful of self-deception, receives the promise of the angel in her will: 'Be it unto me according to thy word.'

It is Luke also who, in his accounts of the resurrection appearances, provides the counterpart to the fallen body of Adam by pointing, even more clearly than John, and unlike either Mark or Matthew, to the nature of Christ's risen body (see Luke 24:39-43 and Acts 10:41, where references to Jesus eating food are explicit), while he is equally concerned with the function of Scripture in our understanding of that body.

> And it came to pass, while they communed together and reasoned,
> Jesus himself drew near and went with him. But their eyes were
> held that they might not recognize him.

Then, after the two disciples had told their tale, Jesus, 'beginning at Moses and all the prophets . . . expounded to them in all the scriptures the things concerning himself.' And later, when 'their eyes were opened' – that is, their spiritual eyes, the exact opposite of the opening of the eyes of Adam and Eve – they said to each other: 'Did not our heart burn within us while . . . he opened to us the scriptures?' (Luke 24:13-35).

Luke follows this story immediately with an appearance of Jesus to all the disciples when 'they were terrified and afraid, and supposed they had seen a spirit'. And only when Jesus has shown them that he has flesh and bones, but of such a kind that he can pass through doors and appear and disappear at will, and that he is able to eat, but in such a way, it follows, as to transform food in accordance with the character of an incorporeal body, does he 'open their understanding, that they might understand the scriptures' (24:39ff.).

Now what does this 'opening of the understanding to understand the scriptures' mean for us, especially for us for whom the pondering of the scriptures is a fundamental element in our monastic vocation? I think it means that without the risen Christ being present to us, without our heart burning within in as we read, and without our being in a state of fear – the word is not too strong, though I mean the fear which is inspired by love, not the fear which must be cast out by love – our eyes will not be opened to the invisible meaning of the scriptures, and we shall read with our carnal eyes and not with our spiritual eyes. And reading with our carnal eyes means reading with those eyes which are open to the knowledge of good and evil. And nothing renders us more blind to the mystery of the scriptures, and to the mystery of life itself, nor so hinders our understanding of God and of the word of God by which he intends us to understand him, than our judgements concerning good and evil. No, all our judgements must be suspended as we read, exactly as they would be if our Lord himself were present and expounding the word to us, so that our judgements may then have their source in him and not in our own blinded vision. Otherwise our consecrated lives will yield nothing more from our reading than that which is accessible to an academic study of the Bible.

This is not to dismiss the academic study of the Bible. How much we owe to the great biblical scholars! Moreover, our own study, especially of the biblical languages, can provide a way of disposing ourselves to receive the gift of reading with our spiritual eyes, because one must humble oneself to learn and one is inevitably humbled in the process. But the battle between those who believe with unyielding literalness that the scriptures were written by the Holy Spirit and those who spend their professional lives demonstrating that the scriptures – especially those very scriptures which Jesus expounded as revealing himself – were written by mortals at once crass and cunning, is not our battle. It is not whether the scriptures were written by the Holy Spirit but whether we are reading them in the light of the Holy Spirit that should concern us.

I really wonder whether this way of reading, which is open to all of us, learned and unlearned, is not very nearly the most essential work that the monastic life can do for our world?[6]

NOTES

1. *Against Celsus*, 7, 39.
2. The Gnostics, I have since discovered, interpreted 'garments of skin' similarly but they made the grave error of identifying these 'garments' with the body alone instead of with the whole person, a depreciation of the body which aroused powerful attacks from the early Fathers, e.g. Irenaeus (*Adv. Haer.* 1.5.5) and Tertulllian (*De resurr. carnis* 7). Such attacks may well account for the suppression of the interpretation of the 'garments of skin' suggested here. But see n.6 below.
3. I have not attempted to trace the origin of this idea but Isho'dad of Merv (9th cent.) quotes St Ephrem (306–73) as believing the tunics were made of the skins of animals. Isho'dad himself, following Theodore of Mopsuestia, thought they were made of the bark of trees (*Commentaire d'Išodad de Merv sur l'Ancien Testament, I Genèse*, éd. par J.-M. Vosté et C. van den Eynde, Louvain, 1950, pp. 95–6).
4. See Ch. 5, 'The Robe of Glory', in *The Luminous Eye* by Sebastian Brock, first published by C.I.I.S. Rome, 1985, and by Cistercian Publications, 1992.
5. Job uses strikingly similar words: 'You have clothed me with skin and flesh' (10:11).
6. I am indebted to Brother Cuthbert OSB who, following the talk, introduced me to the book *Deification in Christ* by Panayiotis Nellas (St Vladimir's Seminary Press, 1987, £9.95, ISBN 0-88141-030-6, distributed in Gt Britain by Mowbrays/Cassell). This 'extraordinary study', as the back cover justly claims it to be, has a long central

section called 'The Garments of Skin', in which Nellas draws out the theology of such impeccably orthodox Fathers as John Chrysostom, Gregory of Nyssa and Maximus the Confessor on this subject. I have resisted the temptation to incorporate any of it into my own piece, but I cannot commend it too highly to anyone interested in the reading of Gen. 3:21 suggested here.

Sister Edmée entered SLG in 1966. In 1986 she began a study of the Song of Songs, involving the study of Hebrew, on which 'Spiritual Reading' depends for its main point.

Poverty in the Early Celtic Church

MARY DODD, OBLATE SISTER SLG

Anyone who visits Wales, or even glances at a map of the Principality, cannot fail to be struck by the frequency with which the prefix *'llan'* occurs in place names. This word, which means 'enclosure', came to be used specifically of a monastic enclosure and the buildings within it. It gives an indication of the extent of the monastic settlements which once existed in Wales, and which sprang up in the fifth and sixth centuries as part of a general movement which extended over the whole of those parts of Britain which had so far succeeded in escaping the fury of the Saxon invader.

Christianity had come to Britain in Roman times, possibly brought back by British soldiers serving in the Roman army. Tertullian, writing from Carthage in AD200, refers to *'Britannorum inaccessa Romanis loca Christo vero subdita'* ('also places in Britain which, though inaccessible to the Romans, have yielded to Christ'). This is confirmed by two references in Origen (writing in about 240) to Christianity in Britain. Thus there must have been from the earliest Christian times contact between the Eastern and the Celtic Churches, and the latter could not have failed to be influenced by the specifically Eastern concept of monasticism. This influence is said to have reached Britain through southern France and Aquitaine, but however it came, it was primarily a literary influence and, as Mrs Chadwick writes, 'It may safely be claimed that the special form of sanctity practised by the saints of the Celtic Church – poverty, asceticism, solitude, contemplation – could never have become a widespread movement without the communion and stimulus which they derived from the

early Church through the written word.'[1] Indeed, the parallels
between early Celtic monasticism and that of the Desert Fathers
are striking, but certain factors combined to give Celtic monasticism its distinctive character.

It arose in a land saturated, as it were, with the supernatural –
something very different from the highly sophisticated idolatry
of the Greeks and Romans. It was therefore important to show
that the *power* of God, manifested through his saints, was greater
than that of the spirits worshipped by the Druids, and that it
pervaded every aspect of life. Hence the emphasis on spectacular
miracles, in which the aim was rather to show forth the majesty
of God than the lowliness of his servants.

On the other hand, the constant threat of attack from heathen
tribes and pirate gangs brought an acute awareness that existence
itself was only safeguarded by the direct intervention of God, and
so a humble dependence went hand in hand with the authority
born of the assurance of God working within them.

The particular kind of austerity practised by the Celtic monks
was to a great extent determined by geographical factors. They had
no need to build pillars or to retire into desert wastes, for the coast
of western Britain abounds in small, bleak, inaccessible islands to
which the saints would retire for longer or shorter periods – many
of them ending their lives on islands such as Ynys Enlli (Bardsey),
where 20,000 holy men are said to be buried. Others lived in caves
on wild moorland or forest. The monastic buildings were of the
simplest: usually huts made of clay and wattles, but sometimes of
stone, surrounding a chapel, which might also be of stone, and
possibly a refectory. The monks did not sleep in dormitories but in
separate huts, perhaps on the bare earth. Some of the monasteries
were of considerable size, for instance Bangor Is-Coed, where
there were at one time 2,100 monks. Nevertheless, many of the
saints spent long periods in solitude, and the life never seems
to have lost its eremitical flavour.

The Irish Maeldub is recorded in the martyrology of Oengus
as possessing 'nothing in the world except his cloak and a linen
sheet';[2] St Gwynllyw and St Gwladus wore only haircloth. The
garb of the Irish saints was 'a kind of loose garment without

sleeves, made of linen or wool, reaching to the knees, with out of doors a goatskin with a thin cloak over their shoulders incorporating a headpiece or hood. They frequently went barefoot, though they had sandals.'[3]

There are tales of great austerity in the matter of food. Great store was set by fasting, and it seems to have accompanied any earnest intercession. St Beuno, for example, fasted for forty days and forty nights while St Tysilio was building his monastery. There were always dispensations for the sick and those engaged in hard labour, and there is no mention of St Tysilio himself fasting! Moreover, there are references in Adomnan's *Life of St Columba* to fruit trees and milk; and in Welsh sources to fish, milk, meat, butter, and vegetables, as well as to bread. Even so, it was common practice to fast until about 3 p.m., and until evening during Lent. These rules were always relaxed if guests were to be entertained.

One peculiarly Celtic custom was to wash in cold water in all weathers, and even to remain standing in it for some considerable time. There are references to the custom of rising at midnight, washing in cold water, and then going to the coldest room to dress before kneeling in prayer until dawn.

There is no mention of enclosure. Nearly all the Celtic saints travelled widely and many made pilgrimages to Jerusalem. Most made several foundations, and few remained all their lives in one district.

Monks and hermits alike divided their time between prayer, study, and manual labour, making a valuable contribution to the development of their people by tilling the ground on the one hand and copying manuscripts on the other. It was the general practice for monks to build their own monasteries, as did St Tysilio who was mentioned above. Mrs Chadwick writes of the skill with which not only the stone Gallerus oratory in County Down is constructed, but also the little beehive huts on Skellig Michael and the island of Inisks North off the coast of County Mayo. Cadog, for example, believed 'that it was right that all men should do some manual work'.[4] Adomnan's *Life of St Columba* abounds in evidence of care for even the most insignificant objects. Books were especially precious, and the loving care with which the surviving Irish manuscripts were written is well known. Books were carefully protected and damage was regarded as a disaster. The spilling of ink was equally a misfortune, or the loss of milk. We read of a monk finding and trying to renovate an old milk-skin, and of his distress at its subsequent loss. In connection with the material poverty of the monks, it is interesting to notice that in many accounts of miracles only the simplest things, such as bread, a pinewood box, water, salt, a stick of wood, and – in the case of St David – a handkerchief, were used. It is worth noting that St Columba regarded material poverty for others as an evil and did what he could to remedy it.

The giving of hospitality was, as one might expect, regarded as a sacred duty by all religious, but it was also taken for granted among even the poorest lay folk. Through his *Life*, Adomnan gives examples of generosity commended and meanness condemned by St Columba, and his attitude may be taken as typical of the Celtic Church as a whole.

The austerity of monastic discipline was well known. Entry into the life was difficult and the testing severe. The routine at St David's monastery is recorded by Rhigyfarch: 'They tilled the land all day, using no oxen but yoking themselves to the plough. They worked in silence, and none possessed any property of his own. When the outside work was done, they went in and occupied themselves with reading and writing until evening. Then they went to their devotions in the church, remaining there until the stars are seen in heaven bringing the day to a close.'5

The monks were exposed to constant danger. St David built his monastery out of sight of the sea where it would not tempt marauding pirates, and we hear of 1,200 monks slain by the Saxons at the battle of Chester. But no weapons were used against the raiders, and violence was condemned. A further threat to life existed in wild animals, and against these travellers protected themselves only by carrying a staff.

Many of the saints in the early Celtic church were of noble or even royal families: St David was the son of Sant, King of Ceredigion (Cardigan). They renounced their royal status, but used their influence in the acquisition of land for their monasteries. Generally, private fortunes were held in stewardship, not used to swell the coffers of the monasteries, and so collective poverty was preserved. None of the money seems to have been used to mitigate the austere lives of the saints themselves, but they did not renounce the right to dispose of it as they saw fit.

From the first, enormous value seems to have been set on scholarship. Most of the saints of the period were educated from an early age. St Illtud, we are told, 'was the most learned of all Britons in the Old and New Testaments, and in every kind of philosophy, that is, geometry and rhetoric, grammar and arithmetic and in all the arts of philosophy'. But 'these men were not, primarily, students, and their monasteries were not schools. In following their vocation, the monks made a very special study of the Scriptures . . . although they undoubtedly enriched and transmitted the culture of the age, this was not their primary purpose.'[6]

Spiritual Poverty

The reputation of the saints of the early Celtic Church – particularly people like St Samson and St David – for gentleness and love, arose directly out of their spiritual poverty. There was a real dependence on the leading of the Spirit: nothing of importance was undertaken without the clear conviction that it was in accordance with the will of God. This conviction came very often through dreams and visions as, for instance, when Amon was warned not to oppose his son's wish to become a priest – Samson was five years old at the time.

This dependence was accompanied by utter trust in the power of God. There are innumerable examples of this, and many tales of St Columba's monks setting forth in contrary winds, confident that God would make their journey possible.

More surprising for the period, perhaps, was a dependence on others, shown by the leaders of the British Church in sending to the Church on the Continent for help in combating the Pelagian heresy on two occasions at the beginning of the fifth century, and receiving gratefully St Germanus. Cadog took his monks to Ireland to complete their education.

The best known example of renunciation is probably that of St Patrick, giving up his dream of settling in Wales in favour of the as yet unborn St David. Illtud and his wife Trynihid renounced one another, their family, and social position for the love of God. There is the touching story of St David's monk, Modomnoc, who tried to leave his beloved bees behind for the benefit of the monastery when he himself set off for Ireland. They swarmed on the prow of the ship, and after Modomnoc had three times, by disembarking, got them to return to their hives, St David himself renounced the profit they brought to the monastery and sent them off to Ireland with Modomnoc with his blessing. Family obligations were honoured, however, as one or two stories in Adomnan's *Life of St Columba* show, though many of the saints of this period spent a large part of their lives as hermits.

The virtue of detachment was valued. Columba, for example, did not perform all his miracles in person but was content to use an agent; on one occasion he is reported as saying to his companions at sea, 'On this day it is not for me to pray for you in this danger that you are in; it is for the holy man, the abbot Cainnech.' There are many examples of positions of authority being refused, and they were never accepted except unwillingly. Exile is perhaps the most characteristic Celtic aspect of spiritual poverty and detachment, and it seems to have been general. It was called '*peregrinatio*', but was distinct from the usual form of pilgrimage, involving as it did a specific form of withdrawal. It is defined in the Old Irish *Life of St Columba* as 'seeking the place of one's resurrection'. The ideal is summed up in an extract from a sermon on St Columba's festival quoted in that *Life*:

> God counselled Abraham to leave his own country and go in pilgrimage into the land which God had shown him, to wit, the 'Land of Promise' . . . Now the good counsel which God enjoined here on the father of the faithful is incumbent on all the faithful; that is to leave their country and their land, their wealth and their worldly delight for the sake of the Lord of the Elements, and go in perfect pilgrimage in imitation of Him.

Obedience, as would be expected, was an important aspect of spiritual poverty in the thought of the Celtic monks, and came before fasting in importance, as Adomnan's *Life of St Columba* shows. Identification with all the downtrodden and despised was another important aspect and included taking the part of the oppressed, whether human beings or animals – hence the many tales of animals being protected from hunters, from Melangell and her hare, to Illtud and his stag. St Cadog, on the other hand, was indebted to a mouse who led him to a supply of corn in a time of famine. This recognition of interdependence was also expressed in the sharing of spiritual gifts. Missionary activities usually took the form of a deepening of the spiritual life of people who were already Christian. (There was virtually no contact with the Saxons.) Teaching was one means by which the Celtic saints shared their Christian faith, and important schools were set up by St Illtud, St Cadog, and others. Learning was always seen as a thing to be shared, and Cadog 'always cheerfully received all who were anxiously desirous to pay instant obedience to the commands of God, and gave themselves up to the study of Holy Scriptures'.[7] It was felt that all gifts should be used in the service of God, and St David who, like so many after him from Bach to William Booth, did not see why the Devil should have all the best tunes, set out to convert the Druids and used their gifts for music and poetry in the worship of the Church.

It is important to note, however, that in the Celtic Church from the fifth to the seventh centuries the concept of poverty did not exclude certain activities which at other times were avoided, by some even condemned. The exercise of political influence may have arisen out of the position of the abbot, if he was also a bishop, as a secular ruler; but the refusal to submit, either to temporal or ecclesiastical powers whose authority they did not recognize, or to outward circumstances which their spiritual descendants at a later date would have held to be an expression of the will of God, more probably arose from the national temperament. The most extreme example is that of the Welsh bishops who, on the advice of an anchorite, decided to co-operate with St Augustine and accept him as their Archbishop if he rose to greet them and treated them

with courtesy. St Augustine, so the report goes, remained seated
and accused them of many irregularities, including their method
of calculating Easter. The bishops promptly refused to accept his
authority, and the date of Easter continued to be calculated as
before in Wales until 768. Even people like St Teilo, St Beuno, and
St Winefred felt justified in bargaining with and even tricking the
secular powers with whom they dealt. St Teilo, told by a Breton
lord that he would give him all the land that he could encompass
between sunrise and sunset, rode a stag and thus acquired much
more than his benefactor had ever intended.

Conclusion

The continuity of tradition with the Desert Fathers, together
with their geographical and historical circumstances, combined
to give the Celtic Church of the fifth to the seventh centuries
its distinctive characteristics, not the least of which was a highly
individual view of poverty. Mrs Chadwick writes of 'their gentle
way of life, their austere monastic settlements and their island
retreats' with deep appreciation, and they have indeed an appeal in
our technological age. But these were only an outward expression
of a way of life which may be seen to have an even greater
significance for us. Their asceticism was seen primarily as a
'martyrdom' – witness – and an ancient Irish document, the
Codex Canonum Hibernicorum (known as the Cambrai Homily),
which dated from the second half of the seventh century or
the beginning of the eighth, distinguishes for the first time the
'three martyrdoms': the white (the life of renunciation), the red
(the martyrdom of blood), and the green (the life of penance
and asceticism). It should be noted in passing that the green
martyrdom was more generally associated with *peregrinatio*. But
the life as a whole, whatever form it took, was seen as part of the
spiritual combat which has been the work of monks, hermits, and
anchorites alike from the beginning. It is perhaps fitting, therefore,
to quote in conclusion from a sermon of Faustus of Riez, given
admittedly at some distance from the northern shores which have
been our concern, but at the same period (fifth century) and

on an island retreat which had much in common with those we have been discussing, Lérins.

> It is not for quiet and security that we have formed a community in this monastery, but for a struggle and a conflict. We have met here for a contest, we have embarked on a war against our sins. For it is our sins that are our foes . . . Our vigilance must be constantly on the alert, for this conflict will be without ending. There can be no treaty with this foe . . . This struggle on which we are engaged is full of hardship, full of danger, for it is the struggle of man against himself, and will not end save with the life of man.[8]

NOTES

1. Nora K. Chadwick, *The Age of the Saints in the Early Celtic Church*, OUP 1961, p. 37.
2. Ibid., p. 115.
3. E.P. and E.J. Roberts, *Seintiau Cymru*, p. 86.
4. K.M. Evans, *A Book of Welsh Saints*, p. 23.
5. Ibid., p. 36.
6. Ibid., p. 20.
7. Lifris, *Life of St Cadog*, quoted in Evans, op.cit., p. 24.
8. Faustus of Riez, *Sermi xxiii*, from Chadwick, op. cit., pp. 10-11.

Mary Dodd is an Oblate Sister of the Sisters of the Love of God, following a rule of life based on the Community's Rule. Welsh born, she was educated at Bangor, Oxford and Bordeaux. Until her retirement in 1990 she taught at Howell's School, Denbigh.

The Monastery of St Macarius

in the Desert of Scetis

BY A MONK OF THE MONASTERY
Translated by Sister Jocelyn Mary SLG

The Monastery of St Macarius is situated in the Wady Al-Natroun, the ancient desert of Scetis, about ninety-two kilometres from the desert road that joins Cairo to Alexandria. It was founded in 390 by St Macarius the Egyptian around whom, in order to benefit from his spiritual fatherhood, were gathered more than 4,000 monks from different regions: Egyptians, Greeks, Ethiopians, Armenians, Nubians, Asians, Palestinians, Italians, Gauls and Spaniards. Among them one could meet scholars and philosophers, members of the highest aristocracy of the time, alongside simple illiterate *fellahs*. From the fourth century until today the monastery has always been inhabited by monks.

In 1969 the arrival of a dozen monks, under the spiritual direction of Father Matta el Meskin, entirely renewed the monastery, as much at the architectural as on the spiritual level. Until then these monks had lived together entirely cut off from the world in the caves of the desert of the Wady el Rayyan, about fifty kilometres south of El Faiyum. For twelve years they had lived a completely eremitical life, in the spirit of the first fathers of the desert, with the same simplicity, the same total dispossession of all the goods of this world and all its preoccupations, the same deep experience of the divine love, the same total confidence in Providence in the midst of the worst natural conditions and the dangers of these desert places. This period in the lives of these twelve monks had thus served to fuse them together in the crucible of the divine love and to unite them in Christ in the spirit of the Gospel.

It was this group, then, who in 1969 left the Wady el Rayyan in costly obedience to the Patriarch, Cyril VI, who ordered them to go to the Monastery of St Macarius in order to renew it. The Patriarch received the group, blessed it and assured it of his prayers, asking for the spiritual father the grace to make the desert bloom again and to people it with thousands of solitaries. At that time the monastery had only six old monks and the ancient buildings were threatening to fall into ruin. The new group was also warmly welcomed by the superior of the monastery, Amba Michaïl, who is Bishop of Asyut. By his discernment and humility he knew how to provide the new monks with the climate favourable to the desired renewal.

At the present time [1978], under the Patriarchate of Pope Shenouda III (who is personally concerned with the renewal of the two monasteries of Amba Bishoi and Baramous), after seven years of incessant activity in reconstruction and spiritual renewal, the Monastery of St Macarius has more than sixty monks. Most of them are university graduates, and before entering the monastery, have practised various professions in the world as agriculturalists, veterinary surgeons, doctors, pharmacists, engineers in all branches, and so on. They live in the greatest spiritual unity, practising fraternal charity and unceasing prayer of the heart. They are all directed by the same spiritual father, who keeps the unity of the spirit in the monastery. Renewal is also manifest in the careful rendering of the Office and other liturgical prayers, for the monks aim, as much by outward practice as by assiduous study, to show forth to the Church the authentic spirit of worship of the early centuries.

The Reconstruction of the Monastery

The new buildings of the monastery, planned and constructed by monks with the necessary competence, are on the point of completion. They consist of more than 150 fifty cells (each cell has a room for work, a bedroom, a wash-room, and a kitchen); a large refectory where the monks come together once a day for a fraternal meal; a new library of considerable size; a large guest house with several reception rooms and numerous individual rooms for retreatants and temporary guests. In addition there are the various dependent buildings of the monastery: kitchen, bakery, workshops, farm buildings, etc. These new buildings occupy a space six times larger than that of the old monastery – nearly ten acres in all.

Care has been taken also to restore the ancient monuments of the monastery. This difficult and delicate work has been well carried out under the supervision of the best archaeologists of the Service of Antiquities. These specialists have been very appreciative of the efforts made by the monks in the archaeological field. On their advice, not only has the restoration and consolidation of the historic monuments been undertaken, but also the destruction of all the recent and tumbledown buildings which surrounded and even covered them, especially the latrines whose bad drainage system was a real danger for the preservation of the ancient monuments.

The Agricultural Project

At the request of the monks the Egyptian government has offered them 130 hectares of desert land around the monastery at a token price for them to improve and cultivate, and to establish a professional youth centre on it. Various professions and techniques, besides agriculture, will be taught there. The necessary buildings for this agricultural and industrial project are already under construction a kilometre to the north of the monastery.

Some of the land has already been improved and planted with olives and figs; large cattle sheds have just been built; and the monastery hopes to receive from Providence aid to enable them to carry out successfully this project for young people. The ideal which lies behind this undertaking is to unite spiritual and moral formation with professional training.

Our Resources

Up to the present we have spent almost a million Egyptian pounds without having access to any capital sum or being in a state of financial security. The monastery has no banking account, it does not collect alms and is not subsidized by any organization. It never makes its financial needs known – except to the Lord in a common prayer offered for this purpose – and the money comes to us through daily gifts, according to our needs, often in a way so miraculous that it leaves no doubt that God is taking the responsibility for this enormous work, as much on the material as on the spiritual plane.

Conditions of Admission

The only condition for admission asked of the new candidate by the spiritual father is, according to his expression, 'that he should have felt his heart stirred by love for God, even if but a single time'. For it is the love of the Lord which has united us and which does not cease to direct our common life from day to day. We have no other rule and no other aim than to submit ourselves always to the will of God out of love for him. This divine will is declared to us by his Word in Holy Scripture. Thus our chief occupation is meditation on the Word of God, as much in the Old as in the New Testament. There lies the source of our vitality, of our renewed thirst for God and ever increasing love for men.

The Rule of the Monastery

Love is the only rule of the monastery, love without condition or limit such as has been shown to us on the Cross. This love is at once the moving spirit and the end of all our actions, of all our efforts and all our sacrifices. Most of the monks are well advanced in experience of the divine love.

The spiritual father, who is fifty-nine years old, is the father both of the whole Community and of each individual monk. He has had thirty years' experience of monastic life. It is he who helps each of us to discern God's plan for our life. It is he who takes the place of a monastic rule among us. He is a living rule which adapts itself to each case, to each monk, to each unique vocation, and which does not cease to renew itself and to progress with each monk along the road that leads to God. Indeed the spiritual father himself does not cease from interior renewal, and this renewal is reflected in the whole Community. We are not guided by preconceived principles; it is the Spirit of God within us, especially within the spiritual father, who guides us. 'Where the Spirit of the Lord is, there is freedom' (2 Cor. 3:17). The aim of the spiritual father is simply to live himself, first of all, according to the Spirit, according to this interior divine manifestation, always conformed moreover to the tradition of the first Fathers of the Church and of the monastic life. He leaves it to the Lord to transmit to his spiritual sons, by a special grace, this interior experience of their father, in order that they also may live according to the interior freedom of the Spirit. For this reason he is very careful not to impose his own personality but to let each one develop freely according to his own vocation, his own spiritual temperament. Thus a discerning visitor will notice both the unity of spirit of all the monks and the marked personality of each one of them. It is in this way that the monks among us are formed as spiritual men having an experience of God, and knowing how to direct themselves spontaneously according to the interior light of the Spirit. It is undoubtedly people like this that the world of today most needs.

We do not have any rule of penances or corrections, for charity will itself be more effective than any correction. The sense of being strangers on this earth makes it easy for us to submit ourselves to one another through love for Christ.

The Monk's Day

We do not have a detailed timetable; the greater part of the time is left to the discretion of each monk, according to what is advised for him by the spiritual father. However a first bell arouses us at two o'clock for our personal prayer, each one in his own cell: psalms, litanies, personal prayer. A second bell at three o'clock brings us to the church to sing together, in Coptic, the midnight praise. This is especially the biblical canticles (Ex. 15; Ps. 135; *Benedicte*; Pss. 148–50) which chant the praise of God, Creator of the world. This is for us the most perfect moment of our monastic day. We have taken pains to arrange our liturgical chants in the best way by reference to the most ancient and authentic chants of the Coptic Church. In the singing of these harmonious melodies our voices blend together as an expression of the union of our souls, and it is truly with one heart and voice that we sing the praise of the Lord. All the monks are conscious that in participating in this daily praise, and in taking part in the common meal, we taste daily, by anticipation, the beatitude of the kingdom to come. About six o'clock this celebration ends with the Office of Prime.

Unity of Work and Prayer

After the Office of Prime each monk sets about the task which has been assigned to him by the spiritual father and which normally corresponds with the profession he had in the world. The monk begins his work with his soul dilated by the atmosphere of praise in which he has spent several hours in church. Thus he begins to taste the mystery of the unity between work and the praise of God. If he perseveres successfully in this understanding, work is spontaneously transformed for him; from the occasion of fatigue, labour and curse ('in the sweat of your face you shall eat bread'), it becomes a ceaseless praise of God and means of fraternal love.

All the practical works of the monastery are thus transfigured into one spiritual activity, as much on the building sites as in the machine room, in the carpenter's workshop or in the forge, in the plantations or on the farm, at the guest house or the dispensary, or again in the huge monastery kitchen. This kitchen caters for our workmen – who can number up to two hundred – as well as our guests, who normally number fifty, but can be several hundreds at holiday times. The monastery dispensary is served by several of our monks: a doctor, a dentist, and several pharmacists. It offers all kinds of medical care and remedies to the monks, to the workmen, and to visitors. (All our workmen, besides receiving their wages, are lodged, fed, clothed and cared for freely. We take responsibility for their spiritual and moral orientation as well as for their professional training.)

All the works are carried out under the attentive eye of the spiritual father, who possesses great practical and theoretical experience in the various domains, and in the manner of directing the workmen. He is always ready to give advice, to point out what needs to be done, to admonish and to correct, uncovering the faults of the soul which are shown up through faults in the carrying out of the work. In this way the practical life becomes for the monk an irreplaceable means for his formation and progress, for putting into practice the spiritual principles which he has learnt, of becoming aware of his faults and correcting them. Work, often even very heavy work, is for the spiritual father a means he likes to choose in order to detect the deficiencies of the soul and to correct them both psychologically and spiritually. We have however learnt to know with certainty that the work in itself and its success does not at all interest the spiritual father, but that his interest is always bearing on the integrity of the soul, on its growth and maturity.

We never separate the material and the spiritual orders. The whole of our life, even in its most material details, must contribute to the spiritual progress of each monk and of the whole Community to the praise of God, 'for the perfecting of the saints . . . for the building up of the Body of Christ' (Eph. 4:12). We are deeply convinced that it is by means of the works that we do on earth, in themselves so small and commonplace, that we are bringing our heavenly vocation to completion.

This unity in our life between what is material and what is spiritual is a very important norm of our spirituality. It is because of this that the role of the spiritual father is not limited to the direction of the spiritual life but extends to the whole life, material, psychological and corporal, down to its least details. It is equally because of this that we do not have a strict timetable which separates times of prayer from times of work. Whatever the diversity of our occupations during the day, we consider that we all have only one essential task, to which we must give ourselves constantly, as much in our work as in our cell or in the church: to offer ourselves as a holocaust of love to the Lord Jesus, raising our hearts in ceaseless prayer, and remaining always, even in the midst of the hardest conditions of work, peaceful with the peace of Christ which passes all understanding (Phil. 4:7).

A visitor watching the monks at work would not be able to tell a senior monk from a beginner, or the superior from a simple monk, for the work unites them in an intimacy full of charity and humility. Their movements accord with each other, and they exchange all the tasks indiscriminately, great or small.

The Common Meal and Community Gatherings

Towards midday we gather together in the refectory to sing the Office of None, with its twelve psalms, followed by the only meal of the day which is taken in common. During this meal, the sayings (*apophthegms*) of the Fathers are read to us. The evening meal, and possibly the morning one (for the weak and sick) are taken in the cell, at the time and with the amount indicated for each one by the spiritual father according to his capacity to fast, and also according to the physical effort demanded of him. Thus our common life does not hinder the personal life of each monk.

From time to time the spiritual father brings us together in church for a spiritual instruction. But this is not a regular thing; it keeps its free and occasional character which depends on the inspiration given by God to the spiritual father according to the needs of the Community.

On Sunday evening we meet for a time of shared prayer when each expresses freely what is in the depth of his heart. It is also the time when we offer to the Lord all the needs, spiritual and material, of the Community. We consider this gathering for prayer together to be very important for preserving the 'unity of the Spirit' (Eph. 4:3) in our Community.

The Eucharistic Liturgy

According to the tradition of the Desert Fathers we have only one Eucharistic liturgy a week, on Sunday morning. It begins with the Office of Praise at two o'clock, ends towards eight o'clock and is followed by an agape meal. It is through this celebration of the

Eucharist that our Community is transformed from an ordinary
human gathering into the Body of Christ. Therefore for us the
mass cannot be the prayer of an individual, nor even of a part
of the Community, but is essentially the reunion of the whole
Community, gathered together in church, around the immolated
Lamb, to celebrate his wedding supper (Rev. 19:9).

The Place of Eremitism in our Life

We live a community life but we consider that the full flowering
of our vocation as monks is to be found in the solitary life lived
in the open desert, more often than not in a cave cut out of the
mountain side. When a monk shows sufficient aptitude to live in
this way the spiritual father advises him to go out into the desert.
But even before this definitive going out, the spiritual father can
allow some monks to taste the sweetness of the solitary life for a
limited period, either in a cave or in their own cell.

Our Vocation in Relation to the World

The monastery welcomes a great number of visitors, both
Egyptians and foreigners, sometimes as many as a thousand a
day. Most of them are seeking primarily to receive the blessing
given by a place consecrated by the tears and prayers of generations
of saints, whose names have become celebrated throughout the
world – for who has not heard of Macarius the Great, Macarius
of Alexandria, John the Short, Paphnutius and Isidore, Arsenius
and Moses the Black Man, Poemen and Sisoes, Isaiah of Scetis,
Silvanus, Serapion, and many others?

The monastery puts at the disposal of the visitors monks ready
to listen to them, answer their questions, and direct them in the
spiritual life. Most of our visitors are able to forget all their cares
and problems from the moment they enter the monastery. The
great spiritual joy which they draw from this blessed place enables
them to go beyond everything that saddened them.

Above all, in the summer holidays the monastery gives young
people the opportunity of spending some days of retreat among

us. We try to direct both the spiritual and social orientation of their lives, without in any way attaching them to the monastery or trying to give a monastic spirit to the living out of their daily lives.

Among our visitors priority is given to priests, to dedicated lay people, and to those responsible for Sunday Schools, who come to prepare themselves the better to offer their lives to the Lord in various sectors of the apostolate.

Through numerous writings of the spiritual father (more than forty books and two hundred articles), the monastery plays a predominant role in the spiritual awakening of the Coptic Church. We are also responsible for the editing of *Marcos*, a monthly periodical of spirituality particularly addressed to young people. Numerous sermons of the spiritual father, recorded on discs or tapes, circulate among the Copts both in Egypt and abroad. From now on the monastery will have for its use a very modern printing press which will facilitate the publishing of the spiritual father's manuscripts and the printing of his various publications both in Arabic and in foreign languages. The few articles already translated into European languages have been received with much interest in many places.

The monastery has good relations with the various organizations of the Egyptian government. It is generally known that all our monks have done their military service, and that there are among us therefore a large number of officers and soldiers. Above all, the political opinions of Fr Matta el Meskin are respected for their integrity, their humanity and their responsibility. In his book on *The Church and the State* he claims that politics should be entirely separated from religion. 'Give to Caesar what is Caesar's and to God that which is God's.' In other writings, such as *Sectarianism and Fanaticism*, he warns against the tendency of minorities to turn in on themselves and to despise others.

The monk is aware of the gravity of his responsibility in the face of the sinful world, in the face of the Church in its division and decadence, in the face of young people of today who move farther and farther away from God. He thinks of himself as the representative of the suffering world before God, and offers himself daily in sacrifice, in union with the sacrifice of Christ,

for the salvation of the world. On the other hand all the monks
continue to perfect their formation by serious studies in order to
be ready to serve the Lord, no matter where, provided that this
service is not contrary to their monastic vocation.

Our Monastic Life and the Unity of the Church

Our monastery shows forth in its life the unity of the Church in
spirit and in truth while awaiting the outward realization of this
unity. Because of our sincere openness of heart towards all men,
irrespective of their religious confession, it has become possible
for us to recognize ourselves in others, or rather, to recognize
Christ in everyone. Christian unity is for us to live together
in Christ by love. Then the barriers fall down by themselves
and differences cease. There only remains the One Christ who
gathers us all into his holy person.

Theological dialogue must be held but we leave it to those who
are competent. For ourselves, we feel that the unity of the Church
exists in Christ and that, consequently, it is in the degree to
which we are ourselves united with Christ that we shall discover
in him the fullness of unity. 'If anyone is in Christ, it is a new
creation' (2 Cor. 5:17). And in this new creation there is not
multiplicity but 'one new man' (Eph. 2:15). Although we live
our Orthodox faith to the full with awareness of all the truth and
richness which is found in it, we know nevertheless that in Christ
'there is neither Greek nor Jew, circumcision nor uncircumcision,
barbarian, Scythian, bond nor free, but Christ is all and in all' (Col.
3:11). In this interior agony we would be willing to die daily in
sacrifice for the reconciliation of the Churches.

We have found in the monastic life the best means for us of
union with Christ, and therefore the best realization of this
new creation which gathers men of every nation and race and
people and language into unity of heart and spirit. This was
very clearly shown from the beginning of the monastic life
in the desert of Scetis. The particular charism of St Macarius
was to unite together, through his paternal love, men of very
different characters, from very different social backgrounds and

from many different races. Among his spiritual sons one might see a St Moses, the former Nubian brigand, by the side of a St Arsenius, Roman philosopher and tutor to the Emperor's sons; illiterate Egyptian *fellahs* by the side of kings' sons. And all lived in complete spiritual harmony thanks to the spirit of great charity which filled St Macarius and was transmitted by him to his contemporaries and to his spiritual descendants even to our own day. We hope that the desert of Scetis will once again become a place of real understanding, of reconciliation and of unity, for all peoples of the earth in Christ Jesus.

Sister Jocelyn Mary, the translator of this article, died in 1989. She entered SLG in 1944, and was the Sister in Charge at Bede House, Kent, from 1970 to 1976.

Buddha, Dhamma, Sangha

SISTER ROSEMARY SLG

When I was invited by Mother Anne to take a two-month sabbatical, I had no doubt about where I would like to spend the time: at Amaravati Buddhist Centre, Great Gaddesden, a few miles from Hemel Hempstead. Nuns from Amaravati had visited us at Boxmoor and Fairacres and I knew from that contact and from their publications that I would have much to learn there, especially from the teaching of the abbot, Ajahn Sumedho. I wanted to let it be a real Sabbath, to allow some things to remain undone and attend to what is vital, life-giving. In this I looked to the long and highly developed Buddhist tradition of meditation as a guide to the art of paying attention. Two other factors encouraged me: Theravada Buddhism is non-theistic, reverently agnostic about ultimate answers of any kind, so I would not need to either defend or compromise my own position; and it is nothing if not monastic. I felt intuitively that I would be at home with their silence and their life-style, and this indeed proved to be the case.

Mindfulness

If there is one word which sums up the teaching given at Amaravati it is 'mindfulness', the practice of attention to the present moment, awareness shorn of projections. This is not unlike the 'practice of the presence of God' associated with Brother Lawrence, or that clear-sightedness desired by Van Gogh who longed to see a cornfield merely, and marvellously, as a cornfield.

Mindfulness is a deceptively simply discipline. It is not

dependent on particular techniques or conditions, nor confined
to the time of formal meditation. It requires only enough hopeful
faith not to be discouraged when the mind wanders off, gets bored,
and bolts into the blue. Very often the breath, in its natural rhythm,
is taken as the focus for attention. The very dullness of that makes
one notice both how constantly the mind flits about and that what
we perceive is itself changing. Perseverance bears fruit in direct
insight into the nature of what is there and this gives rise to serenity.
It is no longer necessary to be so anxious. It is possible to live at
peace with oneself, and so to live wholeheartedly. Mindfulness is
as much a matter of the heart as the mind and, I was told, 'the
whole practice takes place within the body'.

> There is, monks, this one way to the purification of beings, for the
> overcoming of sorrow and distress, for the disappearance of pain
> and sadness, for the gaining of the right path, for the realization of
> Nibbana: – that is to say the four foundations of mindfulness.
>
> What are the four? Here, monks, a monk abides contemplating
> body as body, ardent, clearly aware and mindful, having put aside
> hankering and fretting for the world; he abides contemplating
> feelings as feelings . . . he abides contemplating mind as mind
> . . . he abides contemplating mind-objects as mind-objects . . .
>
> And how, monks, does a monk abide contemplating the body
> as body? Here a monk, having gone into the forest, or to the root
> of a tree, or to an empty place, sits down cross-legged, holding his
> body erect, having established mindfulness before him. Mindfully
> he breathes in, mindfully he breathes out. Breathing in a long
> breath, he knows that he breathes in a long breath . . . and
> breathing in a short breath he knows that he breathes in a short
> breath . . . So too a monk, in breathing in a long breath, knows
> that he breathes in a long breath . . . and so trains himself, thinking:
> 'I will breathe out, calming the whole bodily process.'[1]

Buddhist Experience in an English Landscape

I did have some misgivings about attempting to come to any
understanding of Buddhism outside of its native culture: could it

be 'the real thing' in the buildings of a former school in the home
counties, where most of the monks and nuns are westerners? Yet
in a bare two months I could not have hoped to appreciate
the meaning of the life and ethos I was sharing in had it not
already been subject to a considerable process of translation. The
complexities of that process are witnessed by the varying fortunes
of the English Sangha Trust which has been trying to facilitate
Buddhist monastic life in Britain since the 1950s. At Amaravati
now there is a sense of purpose and stability, undiminished by
recent disrobings, and it is striking how people from Buddhist
countries as well as westerners feel at home there. Members of
the Thai, Sri Lankan and Cambodian communities from London
come regularly to offer the meal and to practise because they feel
that it is *their* monastery. While I was there, a Thai couple came for
a blessing on their marriage and whole families came for blessing
or to 'take the Precepts'. For my part, I soon learned to be at ease
with oriental customs, to take off my sandals on coming indoors,
to sit on the floor, to join my hands in a gesture of greeting,
and to appreciate the graceful simplicity of the traditional robes
and shaved heads of the monks and nuns. But, more important,
I learned that Buddhist experience is not foreign to me and that a
meadow ringed with oak trees is as good a place as a Thai jungle
for meditating on impermanence.

I arrived at the beginning of September and the onset of
three charmed weeks of unbroken sunshine. We were woken
each morning at 4 a.m. by gentle strokes on a Burmese bell (a
flat bell-shaped gong) and I went across to the meditation hall
while it was still dark, the sky pricked by Orion, with Venus
low on the horizon. I came to relish the sight of the sunrise
and the sunset and the sense of wholeness which comes from
witnessing the beginning and ending of each day. Because the
monastery's weekly 'observance day' is determined by the phases
of the moon, I also found myself using that ancient 'clock': I
looked with wonder at the thin sickle which defines the dark
side of the moon for us, and stood spellbound on clear nights
when she was ringed with rainbows, or on windy nights when
she seemed to run wild in a private heaven, rushing clouds in

her wake. Then one morning the whole hilltop was thick in
mist, and the sun, when it did appear, could have been the full
moon, white and ghostly behind the black, jaunty figure of the
Buddha in the courtyard intent on walking meditation. When
the mist cleared every shrub and hedgerow was festooned with
shining wheels, cobwebs which by mid-afternoon were in tatters,
flying like streamers in the grass.

Watching the moon and the change of the English seasons is the
occupation of the poets: Coleridge taking his infant son out into
the garden to show him the moon, Auden remembering Yeats
on a dark, cold day in the dead of winter, Spenser musing by the
Thames on our 'vnstedfast state':

> Why then dooth flesh, a bubble glas of breath,
> Hunt after honour and aduauancement vaine,
> And reare a trophee for deuouring death,
> With so great labour and long lasting paine,
> As if his daies for euer should remaine?
> Sith all that in this world is great or gaie,
> Doth as a vapour vanish, and decaie.[2]

The cutting of the grass in the meadow, the smell of the com-
post heap, daddy-long-legs and those big garden spiders which
creep up the waste pipes and into the bath, signal autumn quite
as clearly as falling leaves and shortening days. And they may
be a trigger for reflection quite as effective as the four famous
signs which set Gotama the Buddha on his journey towards
enlightenment: his first sight of an old man, then of a sick man,
and then a corpse, jolted him into a new view of the human
state and prepared him, as the sheltered life in his father's palace
had never done, for the possibility of transcending it, symbolized
by the fourth sign, his encounter with an ascetic.

> That time of year thou mayst in me behold
> When yellow leaves, or none, or few, do hang
> Upon those boughs which shake against the cold,

Bare ruin'd choirs, where late the sweet birds sang.
In me thou see'st the twilight of such day
As after sunset fadeth in the west;
Which by and by black night doth take away,
Death's second self, that seals up all in rest.[3]

In another sonnet the sea, never far from our thoughts as in these islands we are never far from the coast, is a metaphor for the same perception, an association familiar enough in Buddhism where the sea is the primary image of *samsara*:

Like as the waves make towards the pebbled shore,
So do our minutes hasten to their end;
Each changing place with that which goes before,
In sequent toil all forwards do contend.
Nativity, once in the main of light,
Crawls to maturity, wherewith being crown'd,
Crooked eclipses 'gainst his glory fight,
And Time that gave doth now his gift confound.[4]

Not to see clearly that birth leads inevitably to death is a recipe for unhappiness – we cling to what is transitory and feel aggrieved when nature is simply taking its course. So at Amaravati we were encouraged to notice beginnings and endings and how we ourselves are part of nature, subject to arising and ceasing: each breath, each footstep, all that is received by our senses, all our complicated responses, will in time go as they have come. In the romantic poets how often this realization gives rise to melancholy: elegies and laments, at best Keats glutting his sorrow on the morning rose whose beauty will fade before the day is out. Not so in Buddhism where, skilfully used, it punctures the illusion that the universe revolves around *me*, and so calls a halt to ego-centric demands and all our consequent discontent. It offers the possibility of disentangling ourselves from webs of our own making and opens up another way, the religious way of going beyond. And this, as one of the nuns commented, is achieved not by floating off and ignoring the world in which we live but by penetrating

to the heart of it. The point is made clearly in a beautiful prayer
for peace by a monk at Chithurst Buddhist monastery:

> Everything is changing,
> nothing is our own.
> Not seeing clearly,
> we perpetuate the disease of the world.
> May we, living rightly,
> come to know Truth;
> That, abiding in peace,
> we may bring peace to all beings.

It is difficult to read those words without recalling St Teresa's
bookmark:

> Let nothing disturb you,
> let nothing frighten you;
> all things are passing,
> God never changes.
> Patient endurance
> attains to all things.
> Whom God possesses
> has nothing lacking:
> alone God suffices.

Monastic Tradition and Monastic Experiment

Amaravati belongs to the southern Buddhist tradition which
traces its lineage back 2,530 years to the Buddha himself. The
name Theravada means 'elder way' and the fact that the monastic
order (the Sangha) was founded by the Buddha gives his authority to the code of discipline followed by the monks. This
is called the Patimokka and consists of 227 rules of conduct.
It is recited aloud by each monk (it takes about forty minutes) every two weeks on the full and new moon observance
days. It would be almost unthinkable to change it and, in the
Theravada school certainly, every effort is made to keep it in

both letter and spirit. Questions of interpretation are decided
by the abbot or the Sangha, not by the individual. The point
is not that the form is ideal, but that it is the given and serves
the purpose of enabling the bhikkhus (monks) to practise and
realize the teachings of the Buddha in a comprehensive way.

The teaching of the Buddha is summed up in the word
Dhamma, 'the way it is', and the way to practise Dhamma is to
pay attention, 'mindfulness'. So alongside respect for tradition
and commitment to it, there is another and essential element
characteristic of the Buddhist quest for enlightenment: go to
your own direct experience. The monks and nuns are asked both
to 'surrender to the form' and to 'believe your teacher only fifty
per cent'. Investigate, find out for yourself.

At Amaravati there is also an important area in which the
Sangha itself, under the guidance of Ajahn Sumedho, is ex-
perimenting. The Buddha in his life-time, and under pressure
from his female relatives, did found an order of nuns as well as
an order of monks, but the Bhikkhuni Order nowhere survived
for more than about a thousand years. In Buddhist countries it
is the Bhikkhu Sangha which alone carries the tradition and is
the third object of refuge for Buddhists. If there are nuns they
are in a very inferior position, hardly more than servants to
the bhikkhus, and permitted neither to 'go forth' in a life
of renunciation nor to ordain. But there is now a considerable Buddhist community in the West and naturally there
are women who want to undertake the Holy Life in its fullness.

In 1979 Chithurst Monastery was opened with 'Nuns' Cottage'
in the grounds, and in 1985 Amaravati was opened as a monastic
centre for both monks and nuns. There are now ten or so
nuns, committed to the Ten Precepts which form the basis of
the Holy Life, but not following the Patimokka and not on an
equal footing with the monks. Sister Thanasanti 'went forth'
as a nun near the beginning of my stay and Ajahn Sumedho
commented on the experiment: 'It works well, but it is under
fire from both sides – the conservatives in Thailand who say it
goes too far, and feminists who want the nuns to be on equal
terms with the Bhikkhu Sangha.' I was impressed by the attitude

of one of the first nuns who embarked on monastic life about twelve years ago now; she said, 'When people ask me about the Bhikkhuni Order I don't know, and that is very peaceful. I did not come to the monastic order to become anything anyway, so it is not a problem. To be free is what is important. It is not important to become somebody, becoming is suffering.'

What the nuns are doing is a striking instance of something which is a constant work at Amaravati: discerning and continuing to honour the essentials of a venerable tradition while living in a modern (and non-oriental) culture.

Living Rightly . . .

The shaved head and almsbowl, traditional signs of Buddhist monasticism, symbolize renunciation and mendicancy and therefore another subtle balance in the life of the monks and nuns: they have left the world, or, as they proclaim it daily in the morning chanting, have 'gone forth from home to homelessness', and yet must have daily renewed contact with people in lay Buddhist life on whom they depend for food and the basic necessities of life. They renounce everything in order to receive everything as gift. When there is the possibility of a new monastery being opened (plans are afoot to do this in California soon) the first question to be asked is, 'Is there a Bhuddist lay community of sufficient size, interested and committed enough to give on-going support?' Lay people who come to the monastery are regarded not as visitors so much as participants with an essential role in its life, whether they put food in the almsbowls, or prepare it, or give of their time, skills and energy in helping to maintain the monastery in other ways. They come in great numbers and with great generosity, and the interaction in giving and receiving builds up a very strong natural relationship. The traditional way in which the monks and nuns repay their benefactors is by giving Dhamma teaching, by talks, but also by the witness of 'living blamelessly', simply being what they are meant to be.

Such interdependence extends beyond human and social relations, making a Buddhist community naturally sympathetic to

environmental and ecological concerns. The first of the Five
Precepts, undertaken by all who seek to follow the Buddhist
way, is to refrain from taking life, which is often interpreted in
the more searching and subtle form of harmlessness towards all
living beings. It is stressed that *sila*, morality, is essential for peace
of mind as it is the basis for living at ease with oneself and one's
environment. If you live innocently you will be less fearful, and
the effect of living well over a period of time is a sense of personal
well-being. I certainly experienced Amaravati as a place where I
could *safely* 'let go' because I knew that no one was going to do
me any harm. It was salutary to realize that that in itself constitutes
quite a special experience in today's world. And I noticed, during
the ten-day meditation retreat for lay people in which I took part,
how our faces changed as defensive energy was withdrawn from
them and we became vulnerable. It was like entering a strange
land or returning to childhood. I began to see such quiet virtues
as modesty, moderation, patience, and the restraints of the Holy
Life in their true colours. Victorian moralism spoilt them for
us, obscuring their inherent attractiveness; there is buoyancy and
energy there just waiting to be recovered.

The Processes of the Heart

Amaravati means 'the deathless land' and what I have said about
it may have given the impression that it is heaven, or at least a
temporary sanctuary from stress, conflict and the confusion of
daily life. It is true there is a peace there, as there is at Fairacres
and in many Christian monasteries, but there is no escape from
the contrariness and difficulties of life.

One of the most striking and helpful features of Ajahn
Sumedho's teaching, following that of the Buddha, is that it
is precisely these things which are our real teachers. 'Are you
frustrated, irritated, riled?' (and monastic life there, as here, gives
plenty of occasion for it) '. . . well, go to it, investigate it, watch
your mind!' Difficulties are not to be glossed over or repressed,
nor is the monastery meant to provide idyllic conditions in which
there *are* no difficulties. Difficulties confront us with 'suffering',

not necessarily in acute form, just the commonplace discomforts which make us wish things were different, and so give us an opportunity to understand it. To study the unsatisfactoriness that impinges on us is already to become a little distanced from it, to be in a position to distinguish whatever pain there is from what the heart makes of it. And this will be a valuable skill when suffering, in the more usual sense of the word, overtakes us. Like the Buddha we may come to see that what we feel is determined less by circumstances, even the most truly painful and tragic of them, than by the insistence of our contrary desires. This is what the Four Noble Truths indicate, saying to us, if we will listen, 'Look, haven't you noticed what is going on?'

We are not going to be able either to avoid suffering or, necessarily, change the processes of the heart, least of all by adding yet another desire to those at work within us. But we can become compassionately aware of our drives and longings, and learn to bear with them without identifying with them or acting on them. We can learn to give time to the heart and its processes; we can wait and allow stillness to arise.

What Is It Like?

Jesus asks his disciples to *watch* and to *stand* as well as to pray. Did he mean something like the watchfulness which is practised in meditation? Are Christian prayer and Buddhist meditation, in some forms, like each other, or even the same?

In my experience, each time of meditation, each time of prayer, is different, and it goes best when I least know what I'm doing; so I am loath to make generalizations. But what I did discover at Amaravati is that the obstacles and hindrances which Buddhists and Christians encounter are the same. Anyone who has seriously tried to pray will recognize those on the Buddhist checklist: wanting something, not wanting something, sloth/torpor (cf. accidie), restlessness and doubt. And the mortal enemies, what Buddhists call 'the defilements of the mind', are all too familiar as well, though we may not be good at naming them: greed, hatred and delusion. So there is a sense in which the task confronting us is the same and all one can do each time is 'kneel down', or sit, 'and hope for the best'. As it is easy to delude oneself and go astray, I asked Ajahn Sumedho how to tell if what I am doing is sound, how to judge my own practice. He said, 'Patience. Are you becoming more patient with the hindrances?'

Ajahn Chah, Ajahn Sumedho's teacher in Thailand, was asked, 'What is it like to be enlightened?' He replied, 'Have you ever eaten a banana? You put it in your mouth and eat it! Well, that's it!' He might have given the question about prayer and meditation similar treatment. Somewhere in such immediacy, and within the range of that word *like*, there is the opening prospect of long dialogue between Buddhists and Christians, holding the tension between continuity and discontinuity, sameness and difference.

So what is it *like?* It is like watching over a sleeping child, or someone whom I love very much, or someone who is ill and dependent on me. Full of love and tenderness, I read her body as she stirs, and follow her every breath, noting the slightest change, wholly at her service. She is oblivious, she is simply there. I could stay with her like this for ever. Sometimes meditation is like that, perfectly combining uncertainty and contentment, rest and alertness.

NOTES

1. Maurice Walshe (trans.), *Thus Have I Heard, The Long Discourses of the Buddha* (Wisdom Publications, London 1987), Mahasatipatthana Sutta: The Greater Discourse on the Foundations of Mindfulness, pp. 335–6.
2. From Edmund Spenser (1552–99), *The Ruines of Time*.
3. Shakespeare, from *Sonnet LXXIII*.
4. Shakespeare, from *Sonnet LX*.

Sister Rosemary entered SLG in 1971, and was Prioress of Fairacres from 1988 to 1990, when she became Novice Mistress.

The Pyramid and the Circle

RUTH ETCHELLS

I grew up the child of a Congregational manse, seeing the work-ings of the Congregational Church (as it then was) from the inside. In my teens, when I was old enough to begin to question structures and the theology behind them, I was greatly seized by the ecclesiology that that church was meant to express. Its fundamental principle was theocratic, *not* democratic; its emphasis was on 'the priesthood of all believers', though retaining, unlike some other churches with a similar emphasis, the gift of an ordained 'ministry' – *not*, emphatically, 'priesthood', a word and concept eschewed except in the wide sense that embraced the whole church membership.

But I left the Congregational Church in my thirties, for a number of reasons: a felt need to be rooted in a more ancient and more continuous and less disjunct tradition, and a hunger for a more disciplined and richer liturgy; yes. But deeper than those even lay a difficult-to-articulate sense that 'authority' was neither clearly located nor well or effectively expressed in the Congregational churches I had known. Whatever the lip service to 'theocracy', the reality looked uncommonly like 'democracy' to me, and a somewhat haphazard and disorderly authority that seemed. I was attracted by the apparent orderliness of the episcopal churches, and by the notion of those who had been 'called out' by the Spirit in and through the Church being invested with a concomitant authority, which was actualized by a special grace given in response to prayer and ordination and consecration services. So 'orders' which were invested with a hierarchical authority consonant with the level of responsibility to which that person was called – authority of no worldly weight at all, profound spiritual weight and *therefore* institutional *gravitas* – such orders seemed to express a right ecclesiology.

Inevitably, so rosy a view has had to adapt, partly to the changes of ecclesiological emphasis even then under way, had I but known it, and partly to the human reality of the Church in any of its forms. I found 'clericalism' was as great a corruption of 'orders' as 'democracy' had been of 'theocracy'. But I recognize now, with greater experience, more thought, more understanding and that sad tolerance that comes from a recognition of our common sinfulness, that these two ecclesiological visions, set in juxtaposition, not only can *neither* claim to be the whole truth, but also are themselves expressions of two of the differing understandings, which currently confront one another in the discussions concerning the ordination of women, of how to be, corporately, the whole people of God.

These reflections were triggered by reading and being asked to review Elisabeth Behr-Sigel's stimulating book of essays, *The Ministry of Women in the Church* (Oakwood Publications, 1991). For she early identified differing versions of ecclesiology as being a fundamental element in the debate, particularly in relation to women's ordination, but also in the whole attitude of the Church to its women members and their proper responsibilities. As we shall see, she also recognized that such ecclesiological questions cannot be asked without raising theological and soteriological issues also; in just the same way, and for the same reasons, that they had been raised by my early search for the 'right' form of church institution. She faces explicitly that dreadful gap between 'the wonder of the true Tradition' of what the Church is and how it is to exist as 'a theanthropic mystery full of grace and truth', and the experience of the Church as an ecclesiastical institution 'composed of sinful people tried and often conquered by the passions, prejudices, ignorances and evils of this fallen world' (p.ix). This gap confuses the issues further, since in it the sharpness and immediacy of the Church's Tradition is lost, and *not brought properly to bear, therefore, on the great issue* currently causing so much dissension in many places, but in particular in the Church of England.

Hence Elisabeth Behr-Sigel, who is 'Eastern Orthodoxy's premier woman thinker', to quote the preface by Fr Thomas Hopko, being challenged in her eightieth year to address this subject as it began to be raised in Orthodox circles, invites her own church, and with it us, her readers of many churches, to consider freshly the issues behind the issue:

> a reflection whose goal [is] two-fold: first of all, rediscover, under the deposits of the past, the authentic ecclesial Tradition about women, as it sprang forth from the liberating Gospel of Christ, and secondly, apply that Tradition creatively to new situations. (p. 11.)

In the Church of England, the thinking behind preparations for the decision on the ordination of women may be briefly summarized thus:

1. What kind of issue is this? That is, what is the status of the question? Is it 'first' order, touching the essential and defining truths which constitute the bed-rock of the Church's identity? Or is it 'second' order, to do with the Church's organization, but not its very life?

   Though a strong minority thought it 'first' order, the view was overwhelmingly supported that it fell into the 'second' category, and that therefore each Province was free to make its own decision on the matter, though with sensitivity to the consequences for communion with its fellows.

2. What are the sources of authority we may bring to bear? The Church of England was agreed that these were Scripture, Tradition, and present experience. There is division as to how these 'authorities' address the subject.

3. To what kind of God is the Church called to offer worship? And what is he whom we declare to the world? Questions here concern both Trinitarian theology, and the language used to express it, in particular male and female terms.

4. What kind of humanity in what kind of world? (e.g., a 'female' world responding to the initiative of God? a world whose divine law is that of mutual dependence?)

5. Liturgically, at the eucharist is the priest a 'representative' of

God, or a 'representation' of him? An 'ambassador', or as nearly a naturalistic picture as can be achieved humanly?

6.   What is the nature of the priest's authority? Is there 'headship' implied in it, and if so, does not this properly exclude women from priesthood, in the light of both Scripture and Tradition?

7.   How far is the present freedom and status of women in contemporary Western society relevant? Is a difference between the Church and its cultural context necessarily wrong? How may we both respond to 'the signs of the times' and yet not be slaves to the transience of cultural values?

8.   How far does the mission of the Church to the peoples among whom it is set lack credibility because on this issue it is perceived as unjust to its women?

9.   How may relations with other churches be affected, and in particular, the furthering of ecumenical progress?

10.   How may the Anglican Communion itself hold together, in a unity that overcomes diversity?

In both these latter questions, there is much thought about a) the principle of 'reception' – testing the response and the effect over a period, within the Church, of any change made; and b) the recognition that 'impaired communion', that which may be the consequence between some Provinces, perhaps even dioceses, of any decision made, is nevertheless *communion* and is indeed what already exists today as the mode of relationship/fellowship between many parts of the Christian Church.

All these questions, some theologically fundamental, some to do with the Church's primary tasks of worship and mission, some to do with current forms of ecclesiology and inter-ecclesiastical relations, have been explored in the Church of England by the House of Bishops, by appointed theologians, by written and spoken debate at many levels, and by General Synod. They have also been laid before the dioceses for their careful and prayerful consideration. How does Elisabeth Behr-Sigel's book help in wrestling with them, aiming as it does to apply creatively to these unresolved issues a re-discovered 'authentic ecclesial Tradition' about women?

I should like to take first what she has to say about the cultural imperative and about the weight that should be put on 'natural order'. For she insists on an axiom which seems to me very important in the context of the 'new age' theologies springing up so fashionably around us. That is, that the 'natural order' is not necessarily consonant with the divine order and must always be distinguished from it. She challenges the notion that, for instance, a properly Christian view of women, in the new order of life inaugurated by the saving work of Christ, should be little more than an 'extension of the sexual order of the cosmos', part of the 'natural order', the relation of men to women tending to appear 'as an absolute in relation to some unchanging divino-cosmic hierarchy' – the 'consequent result of confusing the natural order with the divine' (pp. 25–6).

And just as the natural order must be interpreted in such radically redeemed form as the Gospel inspires, so also must the challenge of current cultures. The present situation of women in Western cultures is of a comparative freedom and status. This is set in a context where almost all ethical absolutes have dissolved in the public perception, leaving only 'respect for the human person regardless of race, sex or social condition'. So, she points out, the disjunction of the current status of women in some churches with their status outside, doubly questions the credibility of the Church in the eyes of the world to which it declares 'Good News' of Christ's liberating power. How may the Church both understand and learn from 'the signs of the times', and yet, in Maritain's words, 'resist kneeling before [its] culture'? The challenge is to distinguish the legitimate ethical imperative from a superficial acculturalization.

What was unthinkable in cultural conditions of one given period can become a moral and spiritual necessity for the Christian whose conscience has acquired a greater degree of maturity (for instance in the setting free of slaves).

The question must therefore be asked: Is there a requirement of conscience based on the Scriptures to change the 2000-year-old tradition of a masculine presbyterate? Or on the other hand, is it just a demand of abstract equality without spiritual roots and whose consequences, if carried out, would scandalize simple souls and divide the Church?

(p. 142)

What she offers is a method, an approach. In these and other questions, she puts both the culture and the Church under the judgement, not of the prevailing value systems either in or out of the Church, but of the Gospel it has been the Church's task through the ages to declare:

> The Church's greatness, her grace, is that she transmitted through the centuries the eternal Word that judges her in her temporal and historically conditioned aspects. In these areas, the Church is not exempt from error and sin and therefore quite open to judgement . . . The *Ecclesia semper reformanda* of the 16th century reformers is not incompatible with . . . the faithfulness to the authentic Tradition.

(p. 156)

It is when, and only when, the Church puts herself under this judgement of that same Word she addresses to the world, that her authority is discerned by those to whom she makes the Gospel proclamation: 'This proclamation is the honour of the Church while at the same time her cross because she is judged by it'; judged by that 'divine Word which sets out the fundamental equality of men and women before God' (p. 36). Standing under the judgement of that Word, she can then with authority pursue her vocation 'to baptize this new freedom won by women so it will not degenerate into anarchy and mere confrontation of selfishness' (p. 158).

And the urgency of this latter task, as well as the seriousness of the Church's failure to put herself effectively in a position to fulfil this vocation, is well caught by Elisabeth Behr-Sigel, who points to the 'struggle for power, mutual oppression and exploitation which disfigures Eve's face as much as Adam's'. Certainly 'there is no salvation by woman as such, as a certain pseudo-mystical feminism seems to proclaim'.

Against this struggle for power which the quest for the dis-covery of the proper ministry of women in the Church can degenerate into, in both the women and the men who agonize over it, is set what Elisabeth Behr-Sigel, analysing Scripture and the Fathers, calls 'the real and authentic Tradition'. For, she says, the Fathers discerned (though they did not pursue the consequences of) the biblical revelation of the creation of *one* humanity, in a double polarity of male and female, 'in the image and towards the likeness of the one transcendent God in three persons'. According to this same 'authentic Tradition' the ecclesial community is called to bring about a unity 'that is in the image of the divine Uni-Trinity': a communion of persons not in opposition to one another, but by their co-operation in love, by conciliarity. And it is this 'being-for-the-other' which can con-front the power struggle which is so much a part of our response, a false response, to these issues, can confront and dissolve it.

We are at the heart of Elisabeth Behr-Sigel's approach, which is a theological one, and specifically a Trinitarian one. She carefully analyses the specific biblical texts which are at the centre of scriptural discussion: the two Genesis accounts of creation, and the Genesis account of the Fall. She looks at the accounts of the masculinity of Christ and the apostles in the four gospels, and notices the role of women amongst his followers as the gospels and the early church documents, in particular Eph. 5:21-32, 1 Cor. 11:3-15, and 1 Cor. 14:34, describe it. She relates their specificity to the broad and profound context of Paul's great affirmation of the new order of human life in Christ Jesus. She shows us how the Fathers responded to these and other texts. She examines in particular the role of Mary, and insists on the active, not passive, role that her free and willing assent gave her in God's mighty plan. In Mary we have a model not just for women but for all humanity in active and joyful and obedient participation in the new order of relationships, both intra-human and between God and humanity. She explores the 'otherness' of men and women as we perceive it socially, biologically, historically and scripturally. She studies the different senses in which at the eucharist the priest 'represents' Christ, and notes that he must also

'represent' the people whose worship he is leading, expressing
for *them* their 'royal priesthood'. All these she elucidates most
searchingly, though with some repetitiveness because this is a
book of essays (and indeed it might well have been more sharply
edited). But linking them all, and at their very heart, is the issue
of how we are to understand the Trinity, and the ecclesiological
consequences of that. So it is to that we must finally turn, for it
shapes that view of the 'real and authentic Tradition' we noted
above, which we must bring to bear on our present confusion.

Elisabeth Behr-Sigel posits a Trinitarian theology whose emphasis is not on the distinctiveness of the three Persons of the
Godhead, but on their co-operation in love. It is conciliarity
which is the movement of this theology, a free-flowing mutuality.
She uses as illustrations several icons; but perhaps her most moving
and lovely image, drawn from Tradition, is of the circle which is a
dance:

> To indicate the circulation of life and of mutual service which
> unite The Three who are one single God, the Fathers of the
> Church used the word *perichoresis*. Its etymological origins suggest
> images of a dance in which, as Metropolitan Anthony of Sourozh
> recently said, 'each person is simultaneously in the place of the
> other: a total unity in which each person, while not being the
> other persons, is what the others are.'
>
> (p.13)

Such an understanding of 'what kind of God he is' leads to the
vocation of the people to be (like Adam and Eve before the Fall)
'towards his likeness': a *koinonia*, a communion of persons and of
local churches in Christ through the Holy Spirit, a 'community of
equal although different persons within the radiant mystery of the
Trinity. All members, both men and women, are turned towards
Christ who saves and reconciles all human beings' (p. 15).

We might take as the symbol of *this* understanding of the
Trinity, a circle. But there is another, deeply-rooted understanding of God who is Trinity, which is hierarchical. We might
take the pyramid as its symbol. It recognizes the force of that

biblical theology in which, when all things are at Christ's feet, he surrenders them to the Father in whose obedience he has been incarnate. The 'pyramidical' structures that follow from such a Trinitarianism, Behr-Sigel argues, were in line with the structures of the ancient world, as was the masculine authority which expressed it: these maintained order against chaos.

The pyramid and the circle. Two views of the Godhead which profoundly affect how we think of the liturgy, how we perceive the priestly order, and how we structure our churches. For instance, looking at the eucharist with a pyramidal lens, we would emphasize the role of the priest in representing Christ, who, himself our great high priest, makes sacrifice of himself. The *special* nature of the priesthood of the priest and bishop is emphasized, their headship, their authority – that which I looked for so long ago as necessary to the good order of the church I sought. We would emphasize also the responsibilities of leadership and the obedience to God, which such leadership expresses and calls forth, surrogate for God, in others. We would stress the orderliness inherent in a chain of authority which mirrors that due to God the Father.

And if we look through that lens which is the circle, we emphasize instead the royal priesthood of the whole people of God. As Behr-Sigel puts it, it situates 'the special priesthood, whose charism is authenticated by the sacrament of order . . . in its proper place: not *above but within the Christian community*.' Those who have received this special mission 'are the instruments of this priestly and invisible grace of which the total Church, laymen and clerics, men and women, is the depository' (pp. 140–1). A theocracy, in fact.

The challenge of this book is that *the question of the place of women in the Church has its origins*, its author believes, *in the tension between these two conceptions of the Christian community*. The pyramidical, patriarchal structure whereby in history and, until recently, in culture, not only was *the Church as an institution* conceived of as quite properly embodying layers of power and authority and responsibilities, but whose upper layers were almost invariably male. Or a circle of mutuality in which each expressed only the authority granted to the whole Church, and held it for each other in God. When we get to such a point we realize that issues of 'headship' and 'authority', and whether women can properly be vested with them, are not relevant, since we are not talking of authority and headship in any traditional human sense. We are talking about an entirely new creation, equal in dignity though irreducibly – and gloriously – different in persons; among whom the Spirit does not abolish differences of sex and culture but transcends them and 'sovereignly distributes his diverse gifts for the edification of the common "spiritual house" (1 Pet. 2:5)' (p.149).

Reflecting on this, I would want to add one further challenge. Just as in my own choice between circle and pyramid I found neither shape – sin apart – expressed satisfactorily in ecclesial terms the Three-in-One I had learned to love and serve, so this opposition here of symbols and their theologies, while useful, is a method only, and not in any sense a definition. We need all the shapes God sends to discern the mystery of what it is the Church is called to be, and they will include the order and authority of the pyramid and the mutuality of the circle.

Pondering these interrelated issues I have found myself continually drawn back to the divine power, through which the mysteries of our faith transcend all the oppositions we urge within the life of the Church. As here, hierarchy and conciliarity must not be allowed to slug it out, but be equally rejoiced in, and equally defended against our instinct to corrupt them, since each is a true and proper way into the mysteries of the self-disclosure of God. He is all authority, power and holiness; he is also the very fullness of mutuality in Love. Similarly, in him is that continuity which keeps unbroken faith with truth: and yet, that which we see in opposition to this, creativity and dynamic for change, is the first law of his dealing with us. He is in the world and yet not of the world: this-worldly and other-worldly; this also is he, neither is this he. He is the very bond of unity that holds the universe together, and all his creatures in their opposing diversities. Yet he is by nature the Lord of the particular, the uniquely individual, the to-be-distinguished-from-all-others which is the *esse* of his creation. He speaks through the word of scripture, unfailingly;

yet he is not that word but beyond and through that word he is the Word. He made the world of time and space his context and requires of us that we live with integrity in the present: and yet the 'end-time' is already inaugurated in the life of the Church. So the oppositions and antitheses go on and all of them find a focus in this question of women in the Church. So, addressing it, we do well to remember that the power of polarity, spiritual as well as physical, is in the holding of the poles in balance: which is beyond us humanly speaking, and there our weakness must be offered for transcending by the Spirit.

But if we allow God to transcend whatever shape fits us too comfortably, and thus to perceive him and the new order into which he invests us afresh and anew and humbly, then indeed this question of the ordination of women may become, as it surely should, 'a question to lead us into addressing the Gospel to the world'. Or perhaps even more searchingly, as Elisabeth Behr-Sigel suggests, 'is not the quest of the status of women above a a call, in a new historical form, for the Church to be converted to the Gospel?'

Ruth Etchells was Principal of St John's College with Cranmer Hall, Durham, until her retirement in 1988. She is a member of the General Synod of the Church of England and the Crown Appointments Commission.

Publishing History
of Articles from
Fairacres Chronicle